Life Is Short...

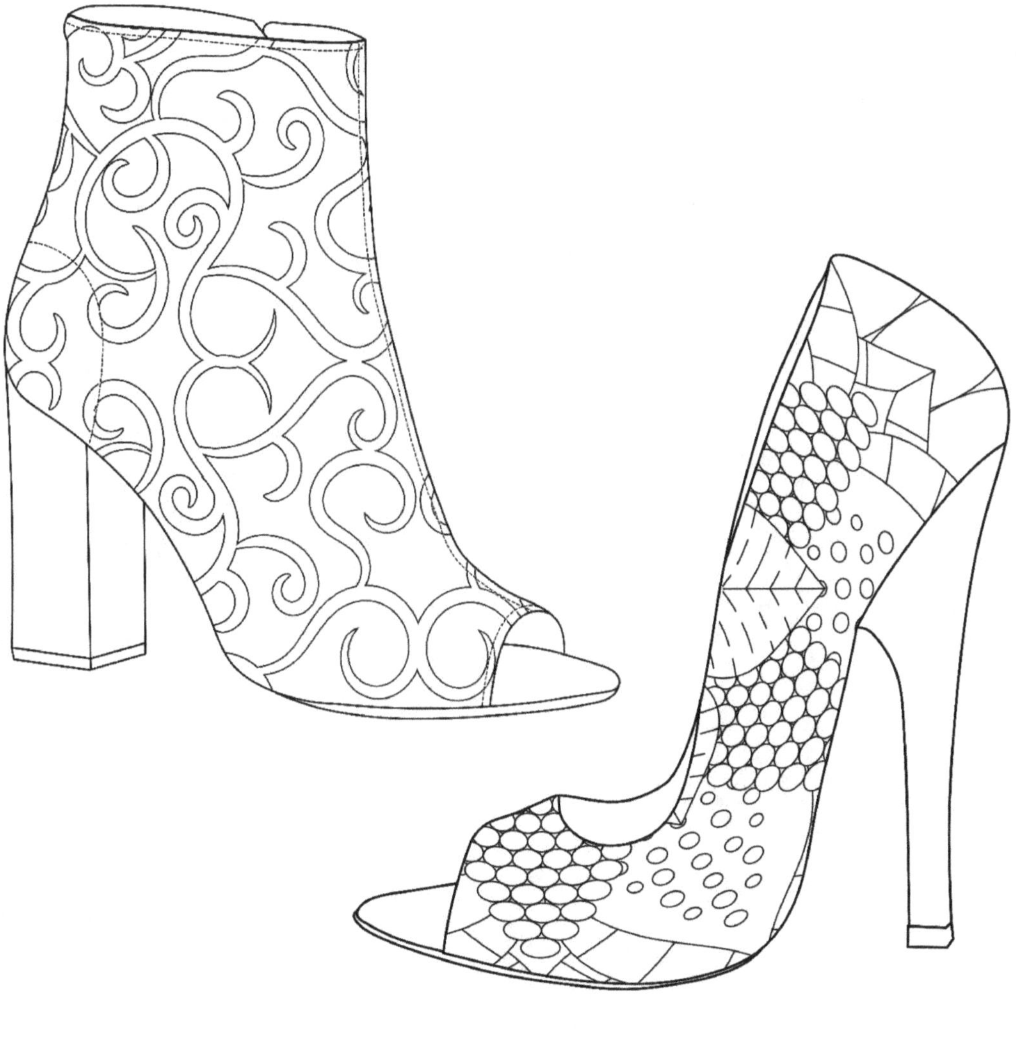

Buy The Shoes!

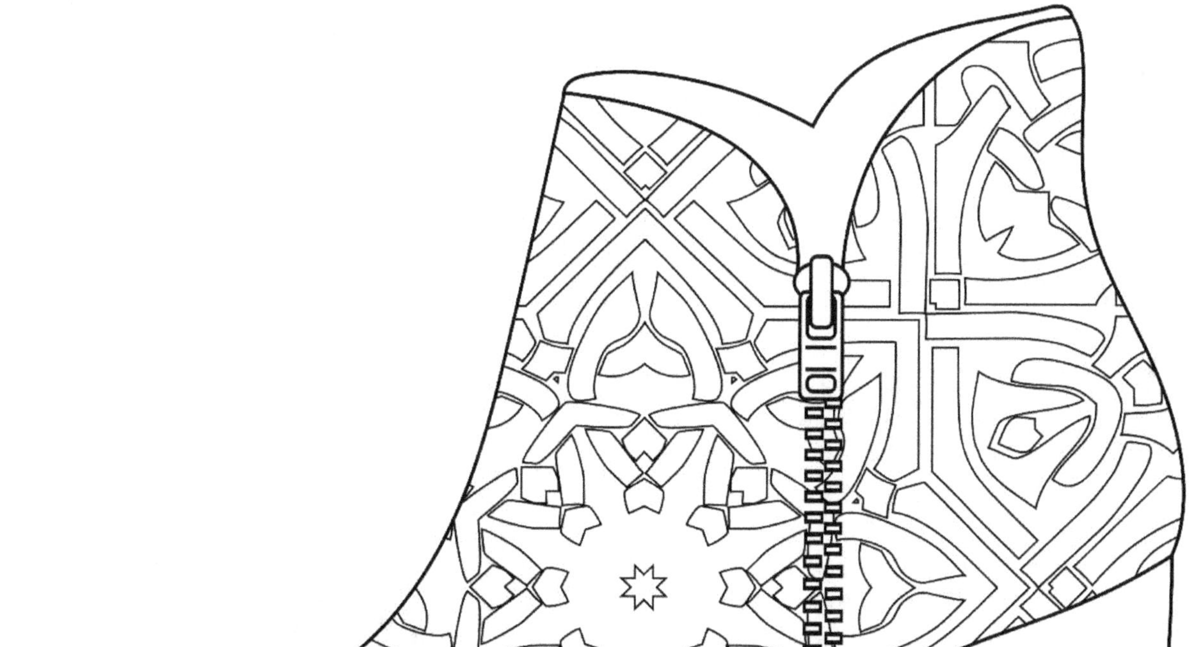

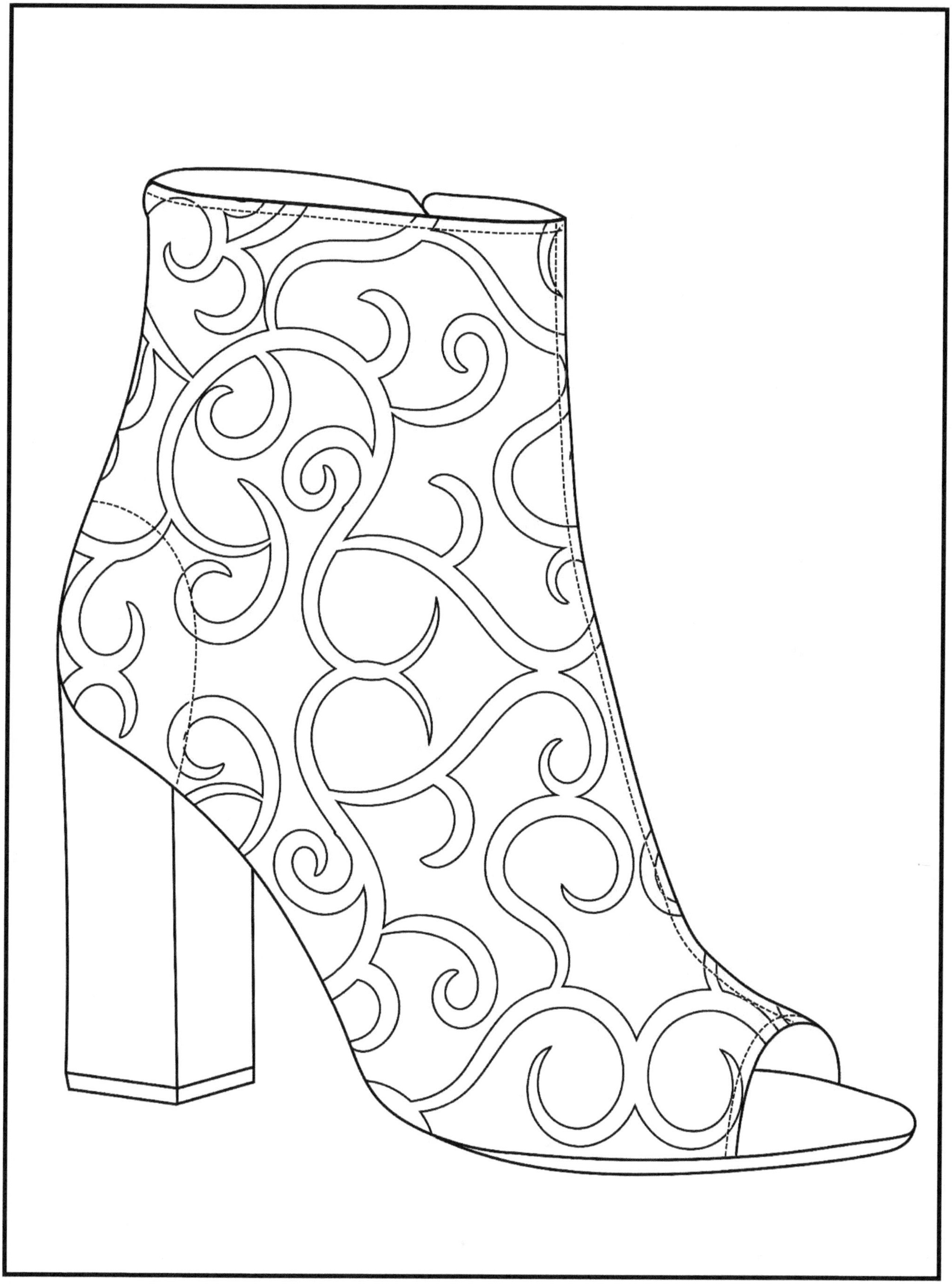

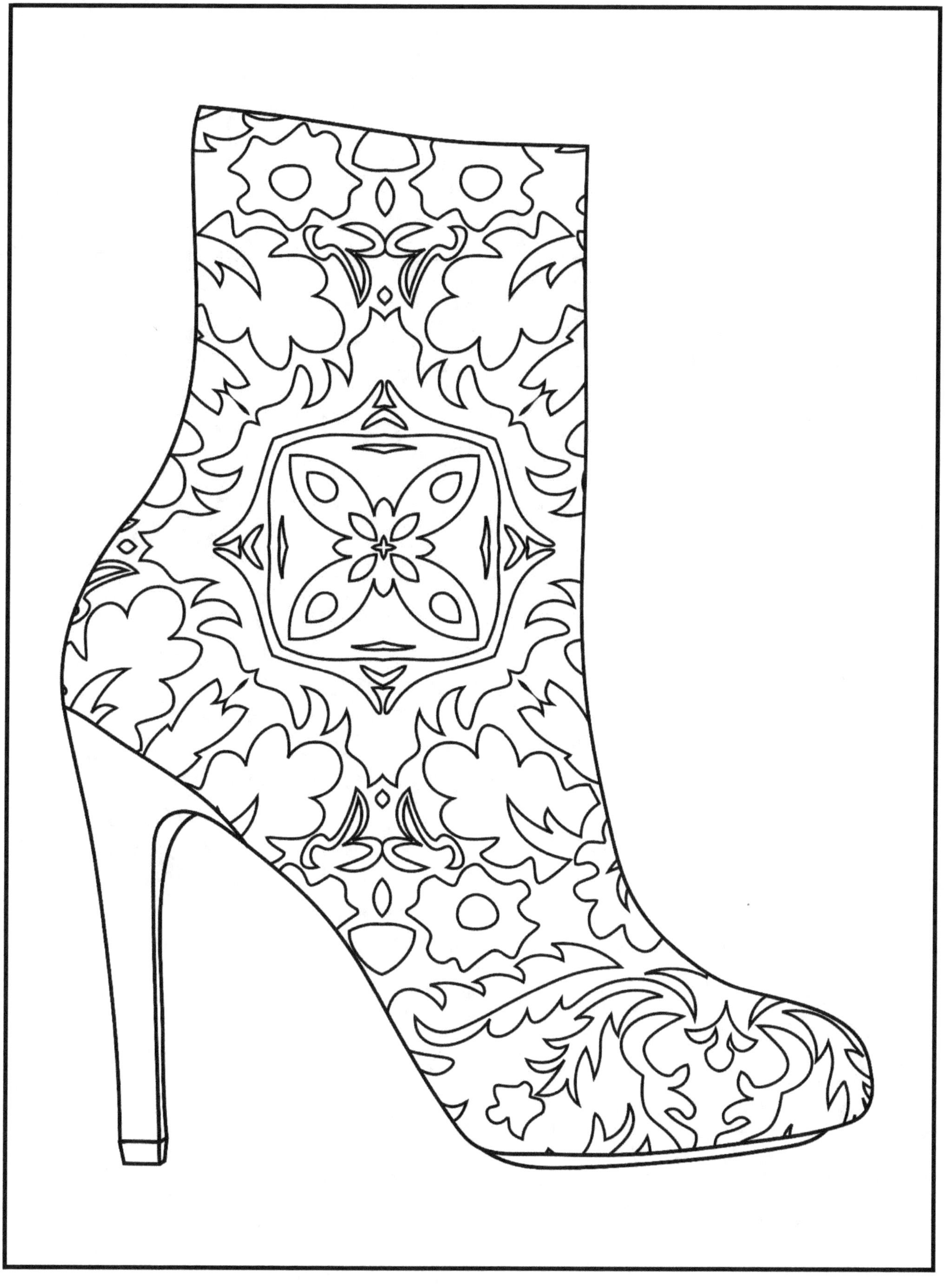

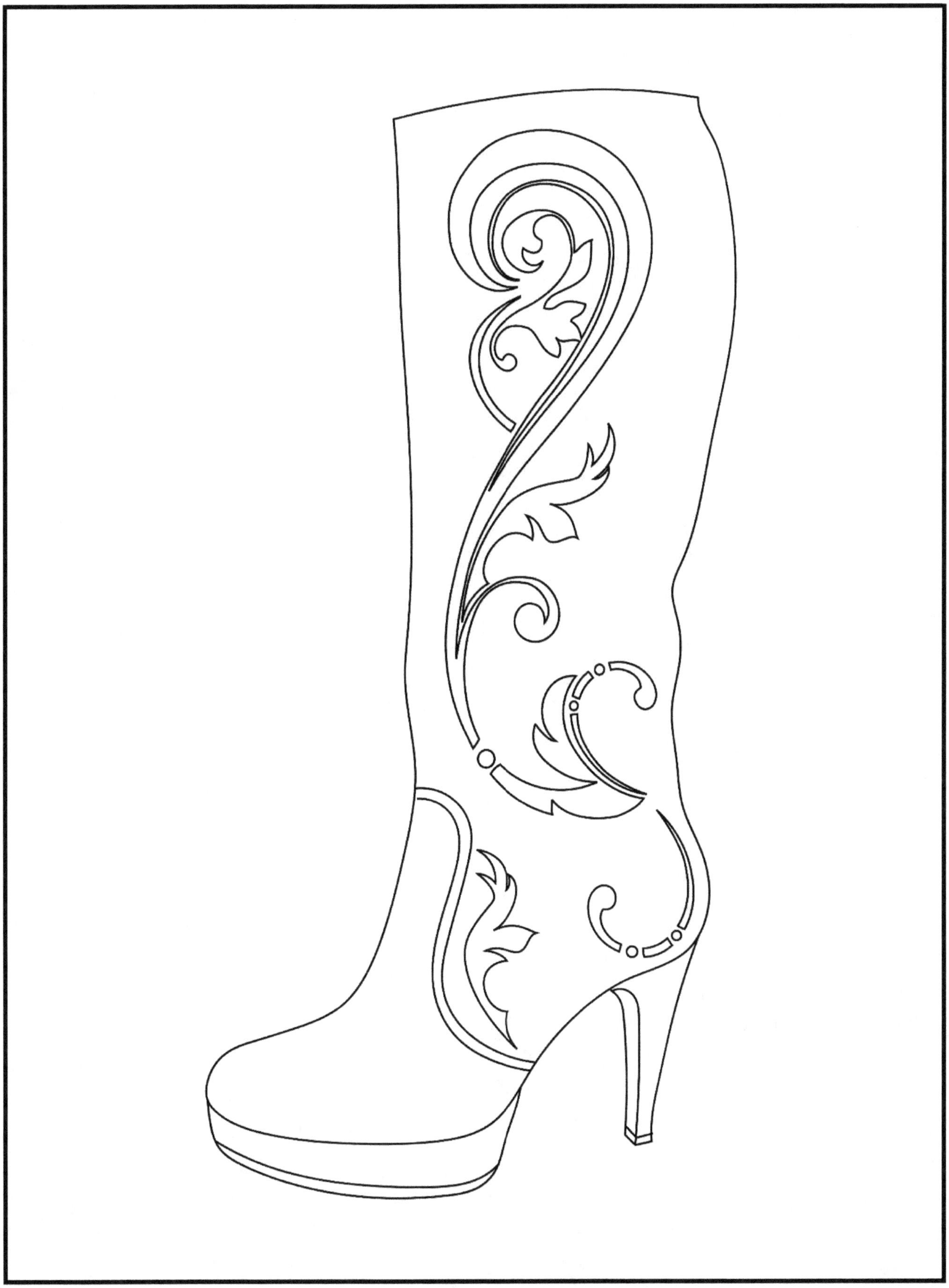

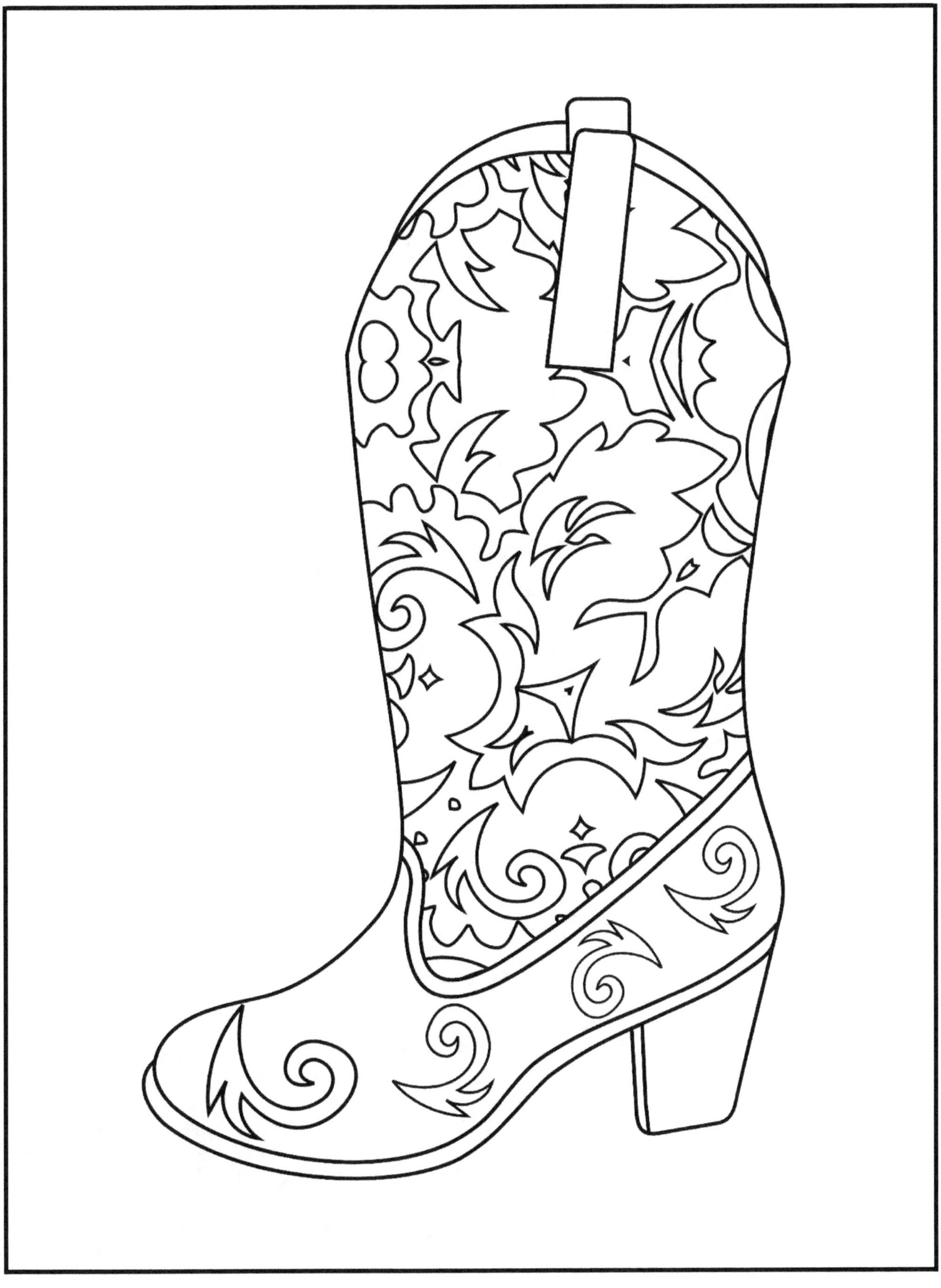

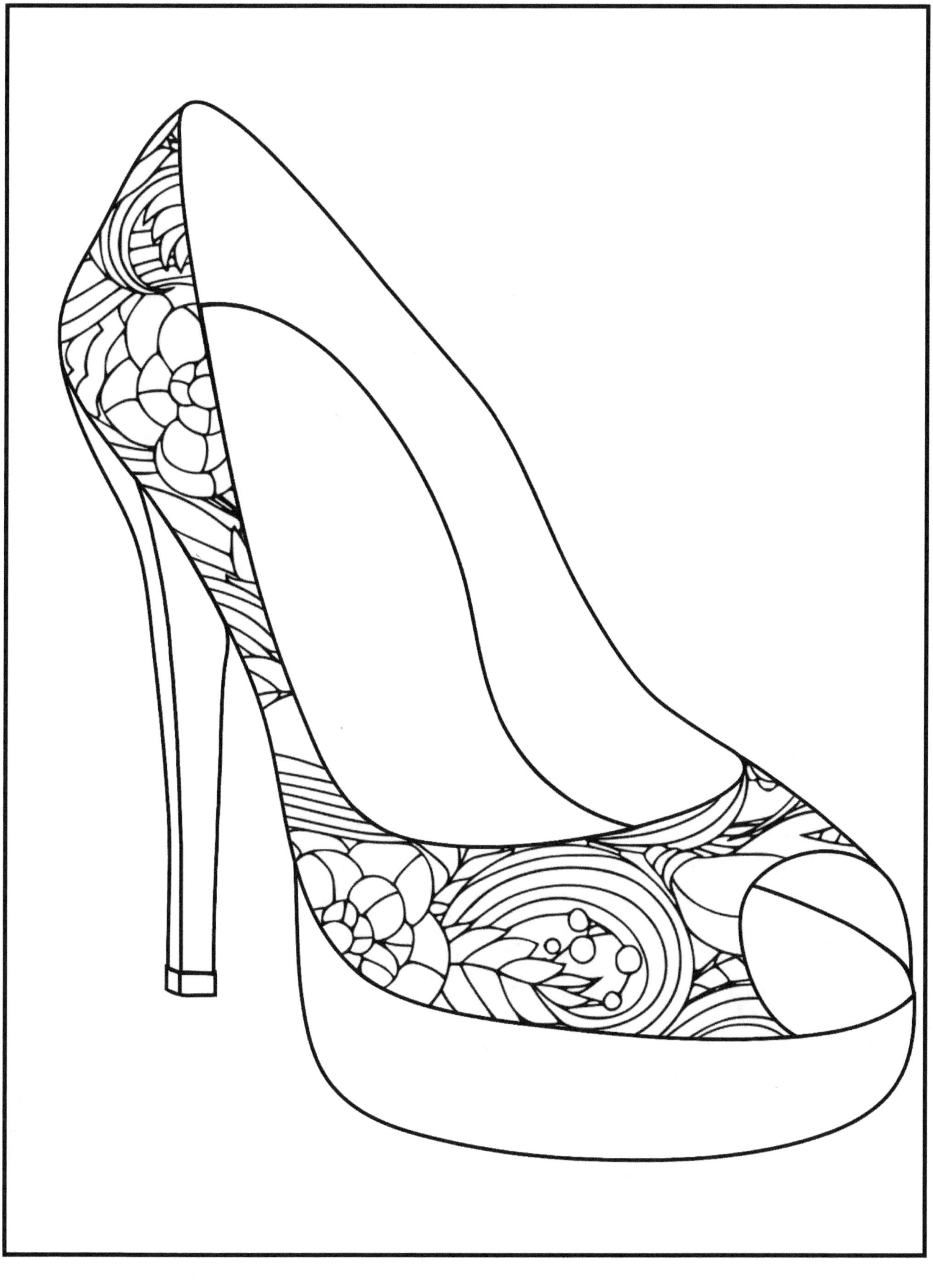

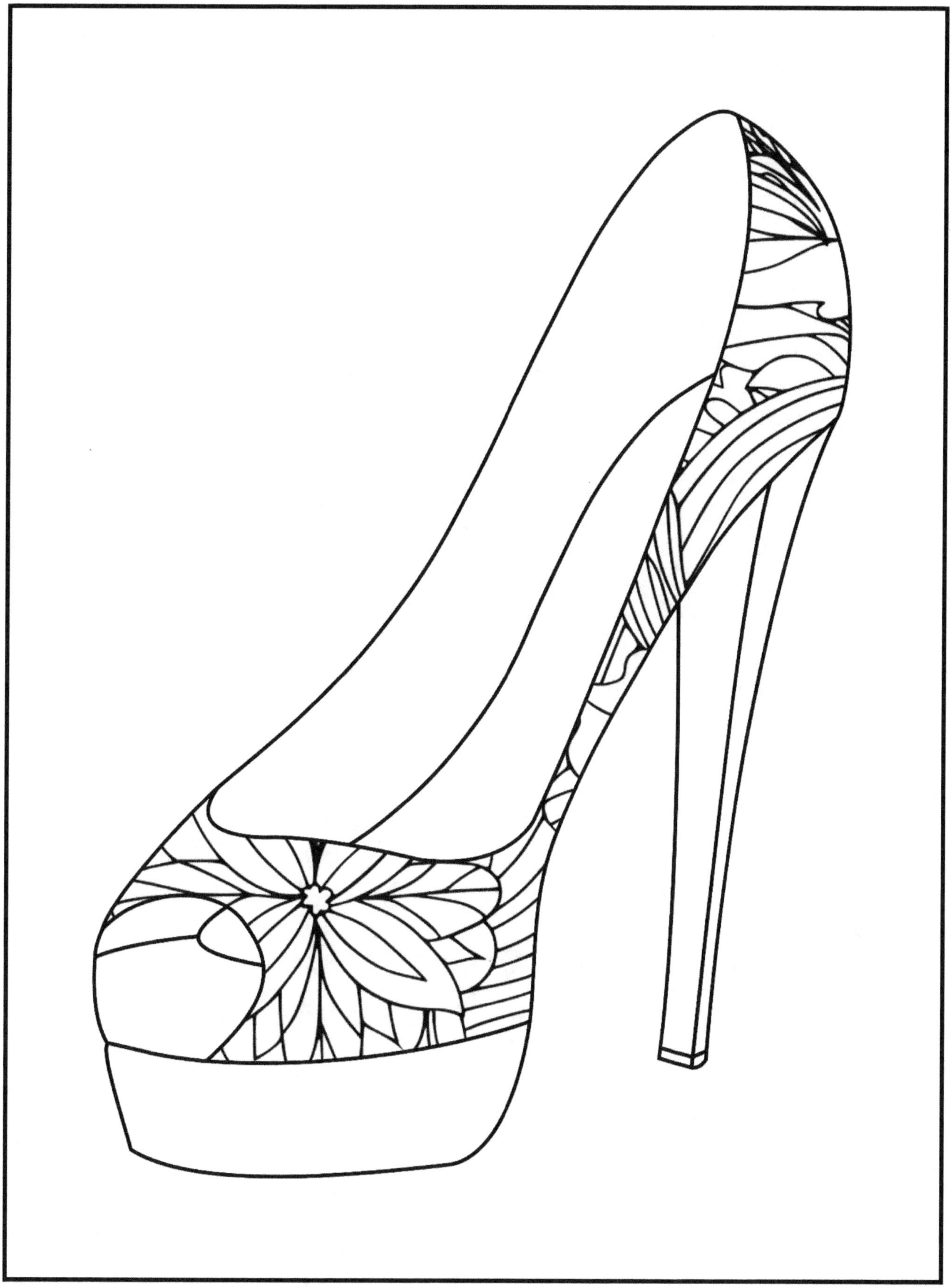

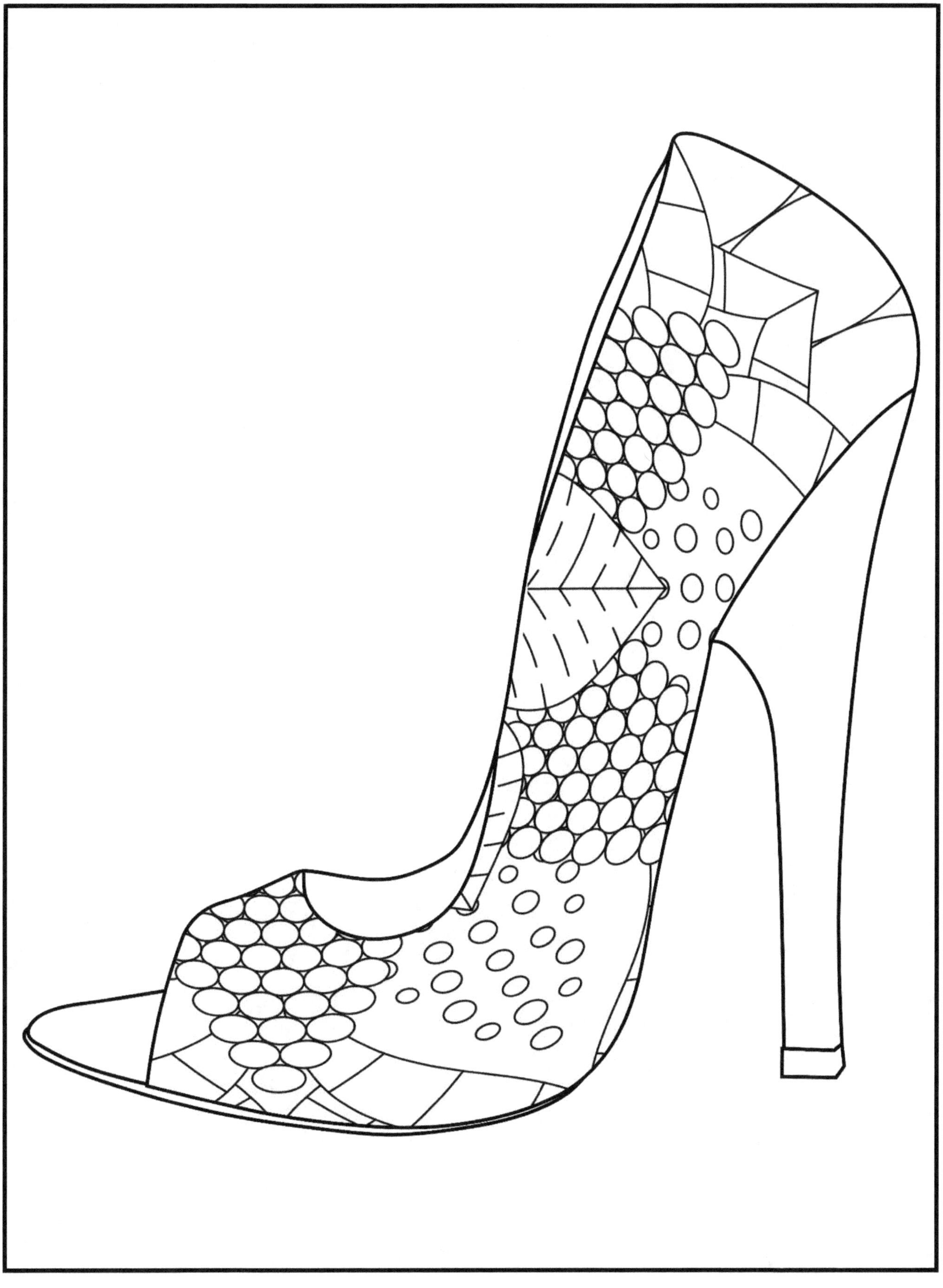

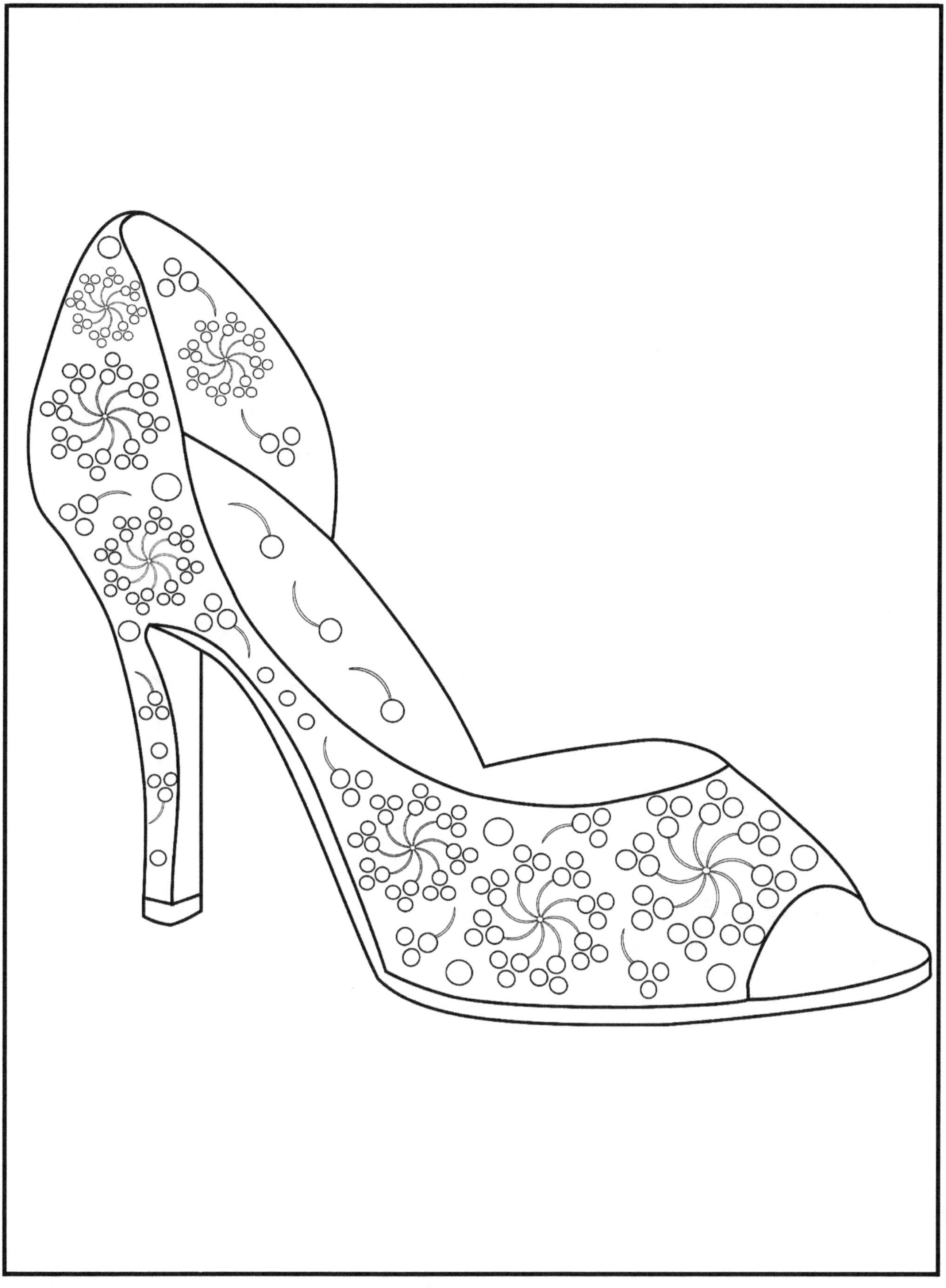

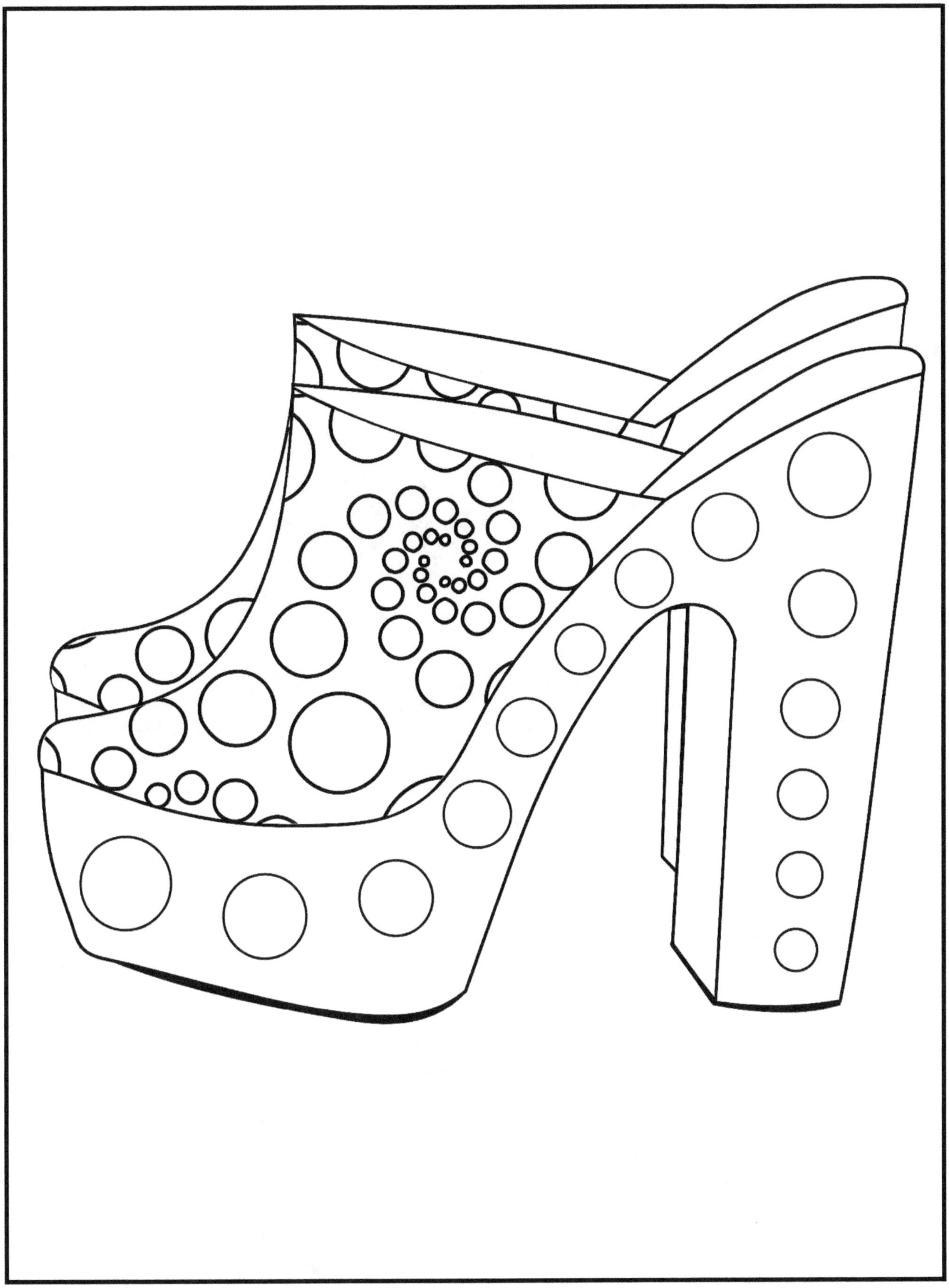

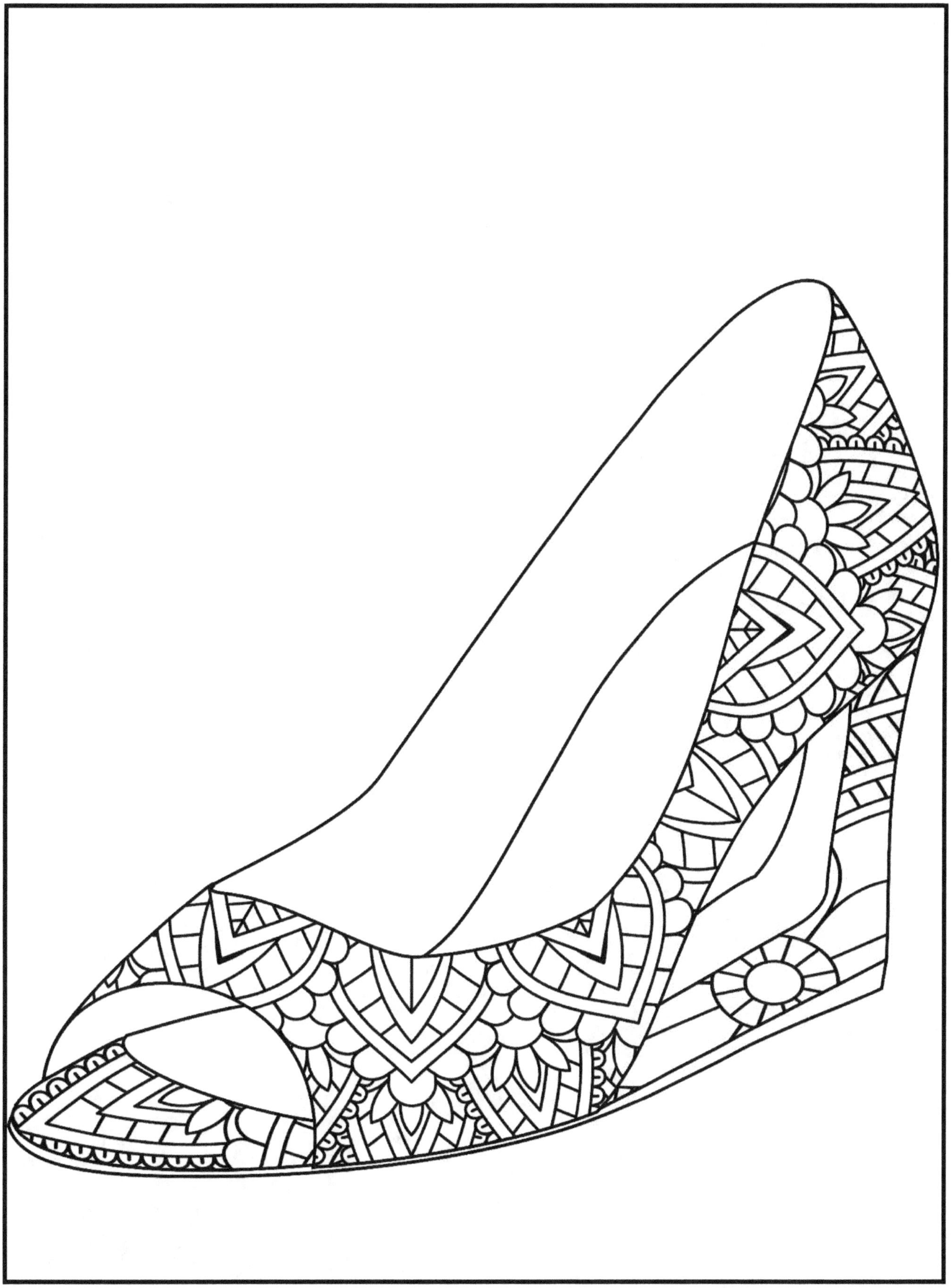

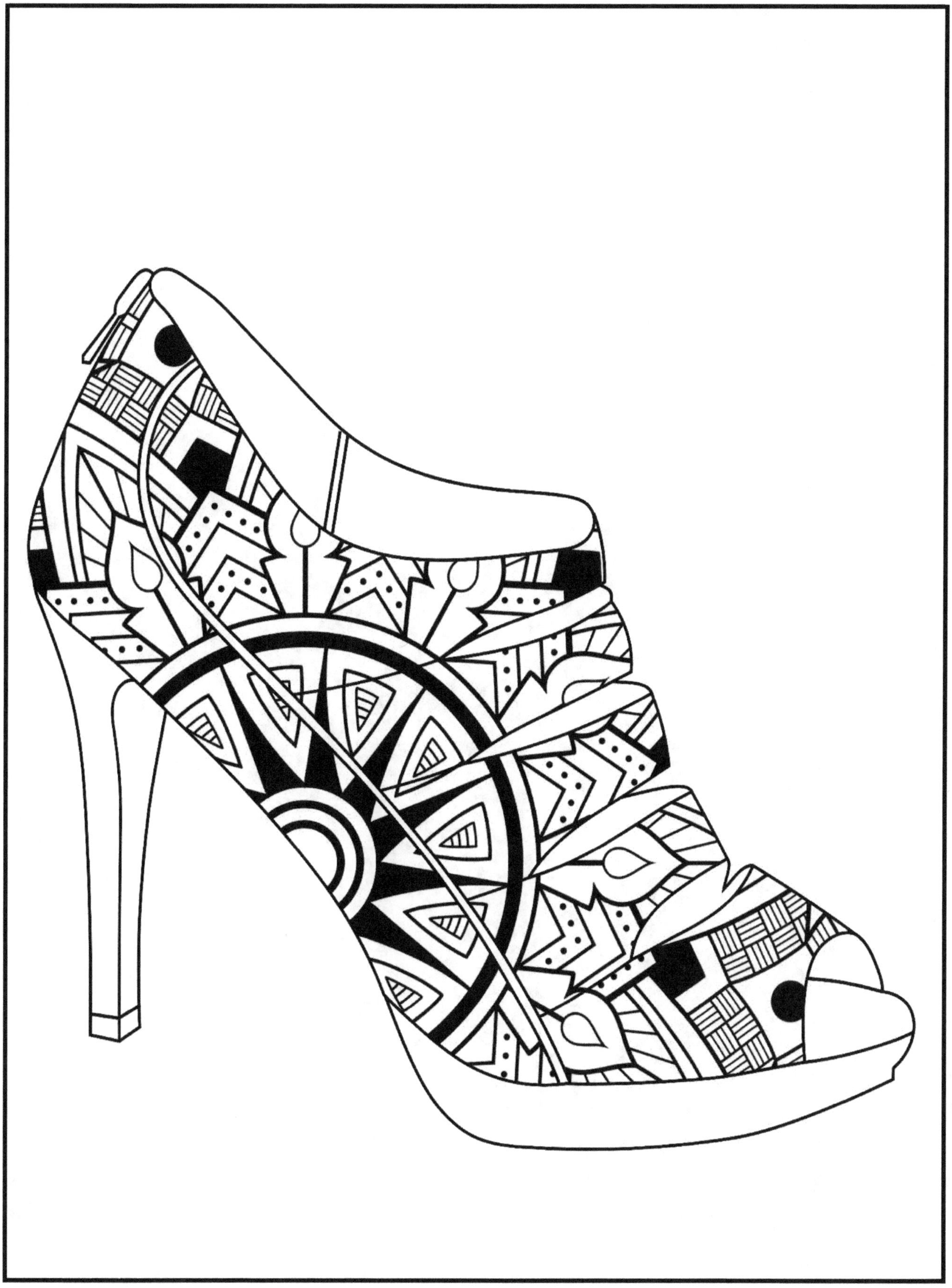

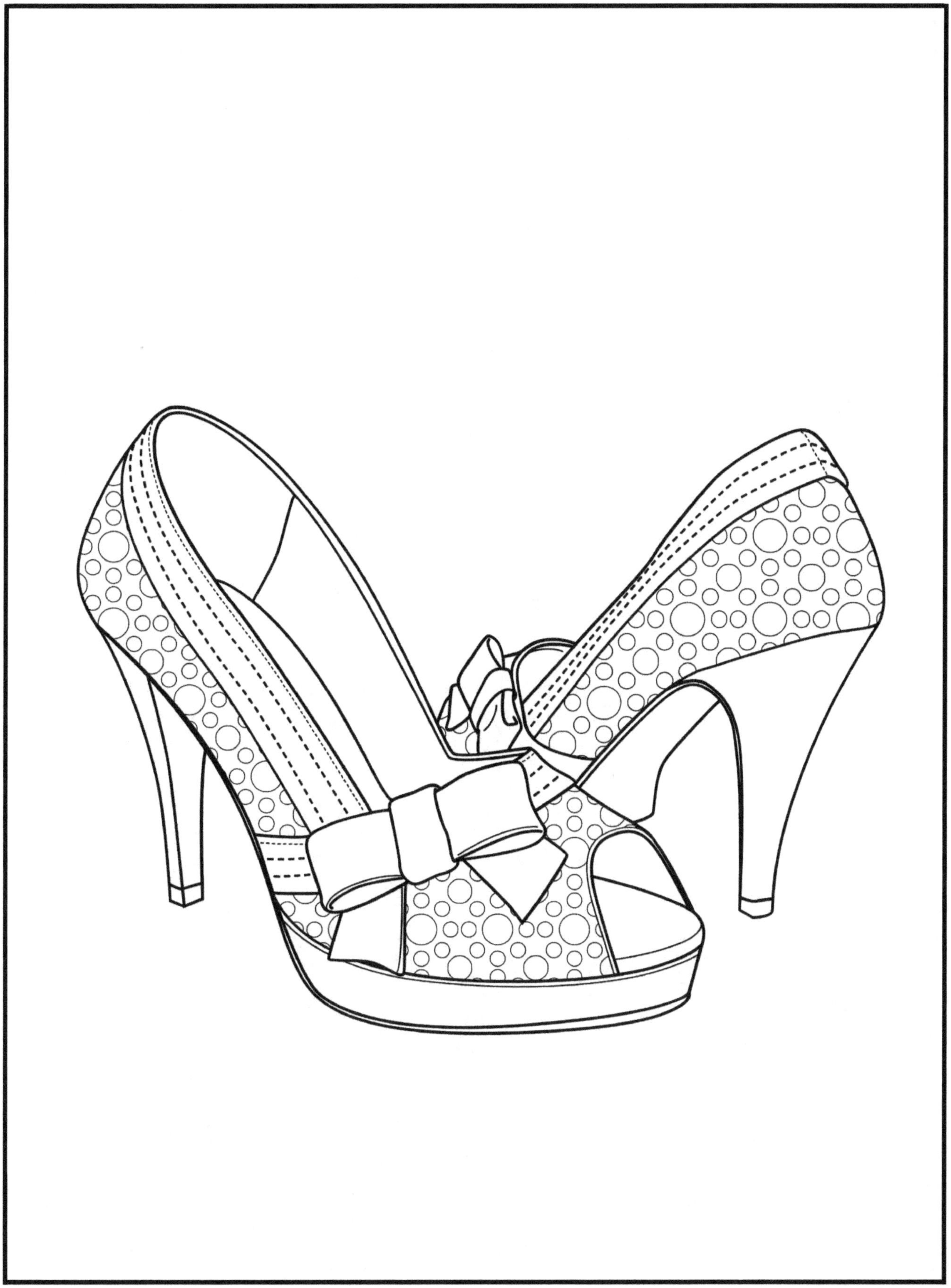

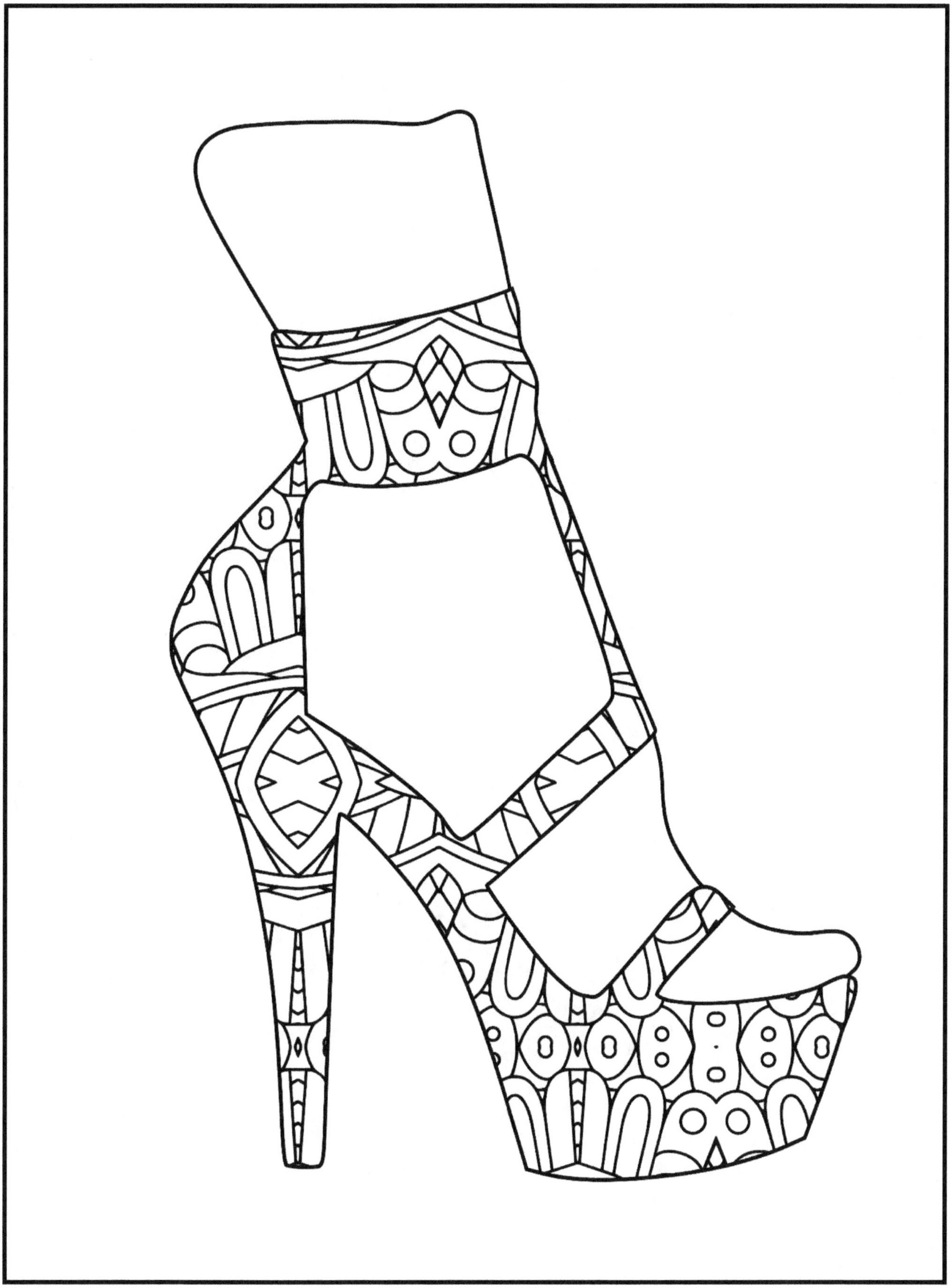

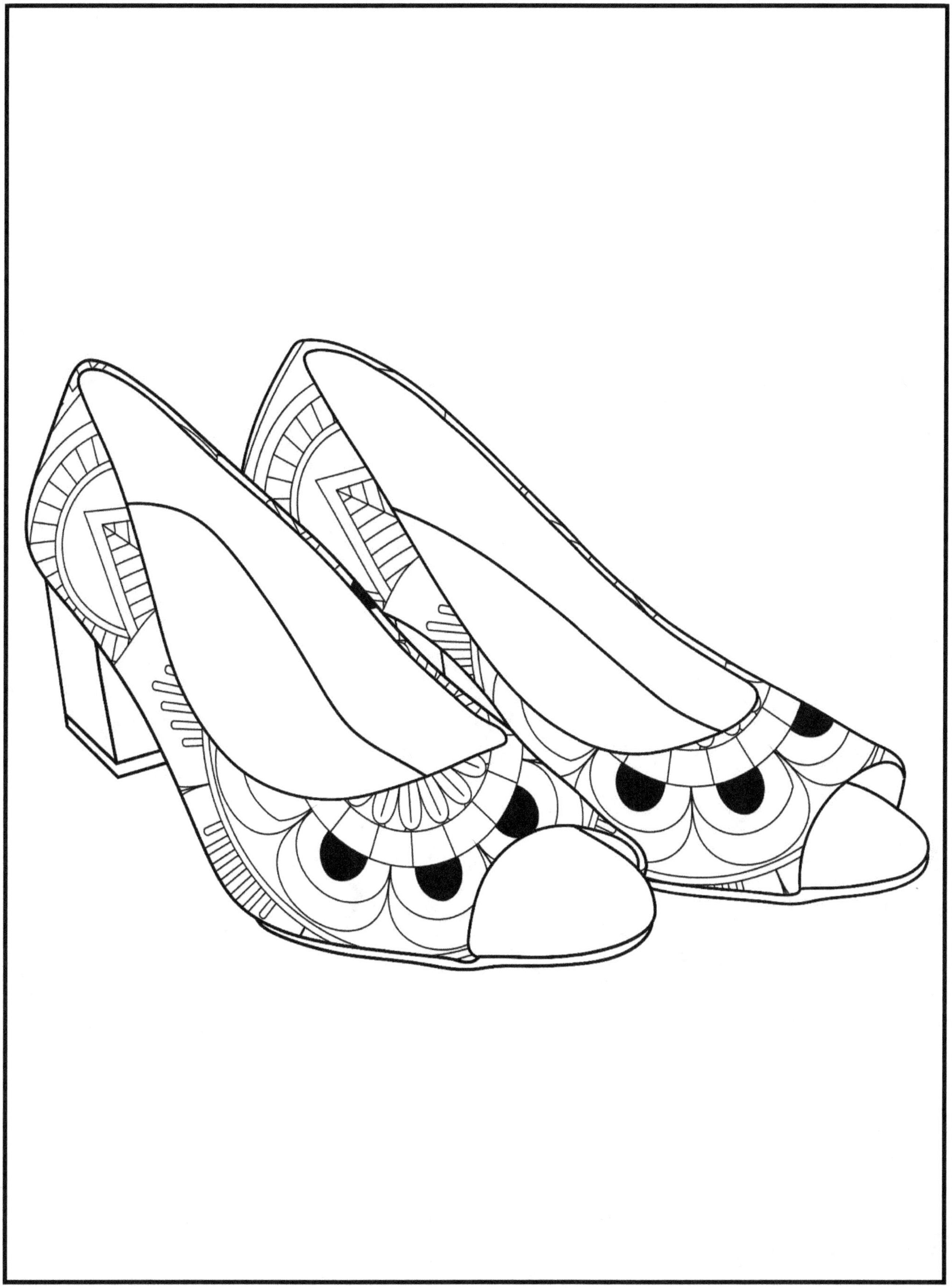

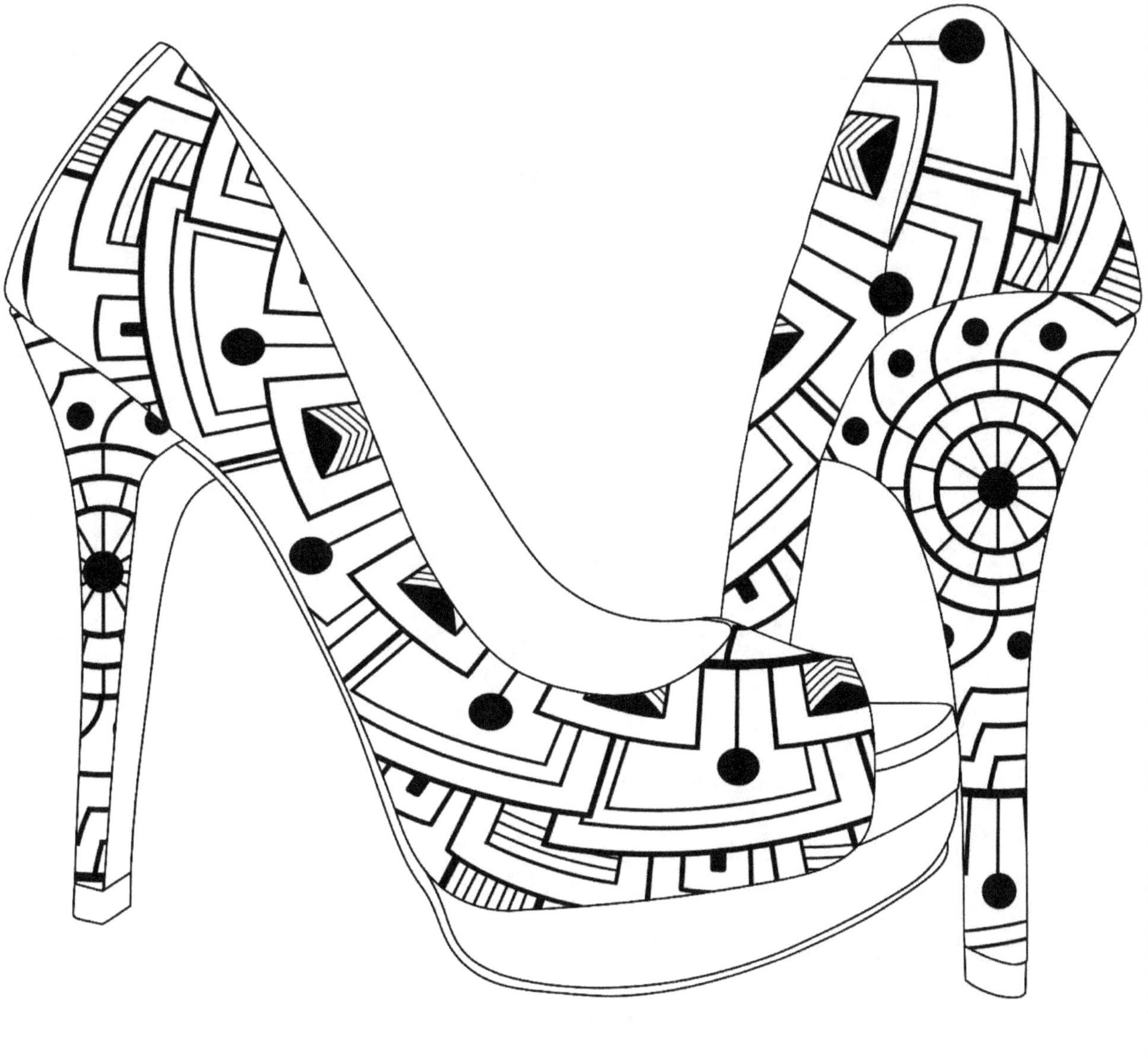

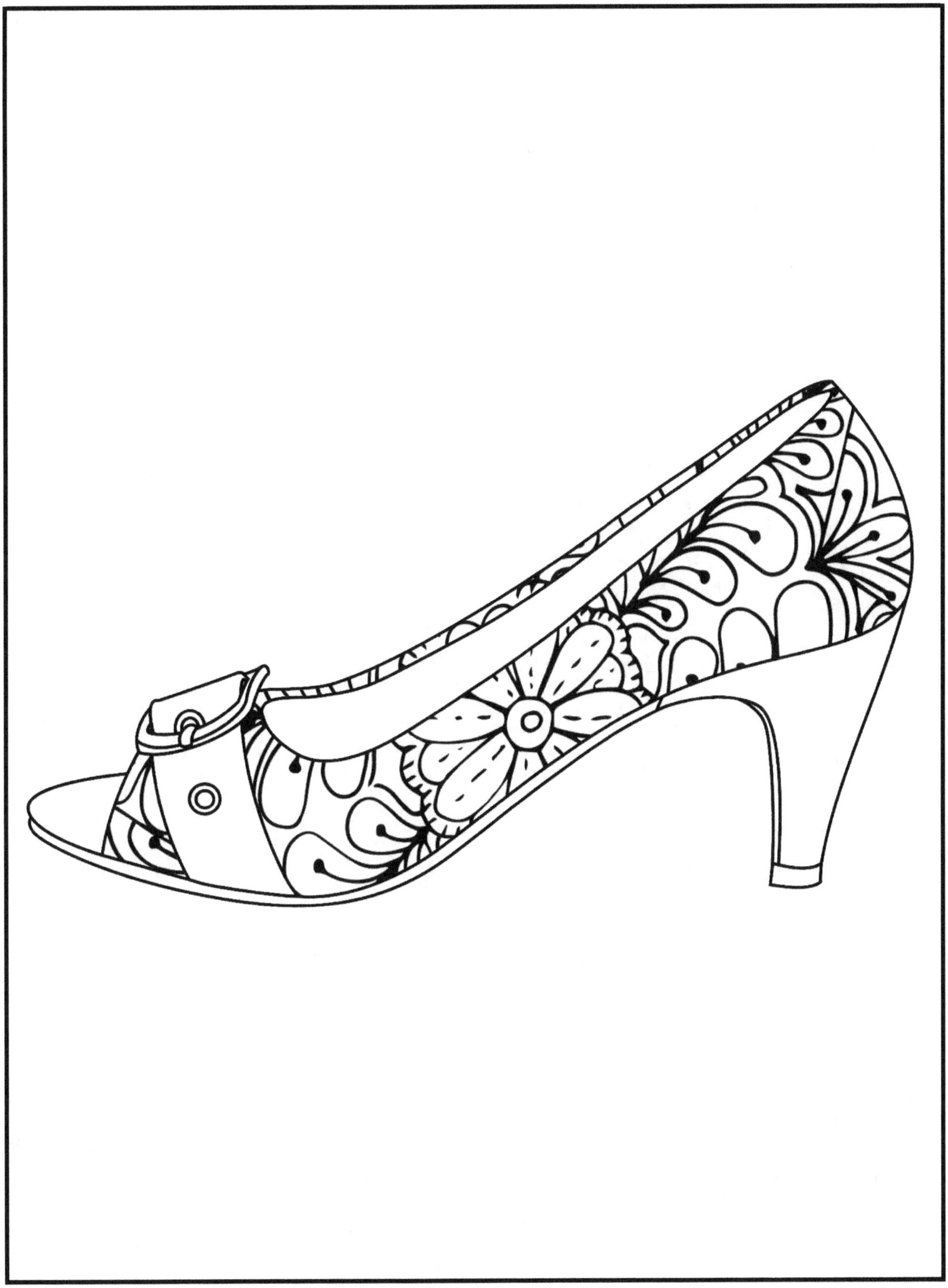

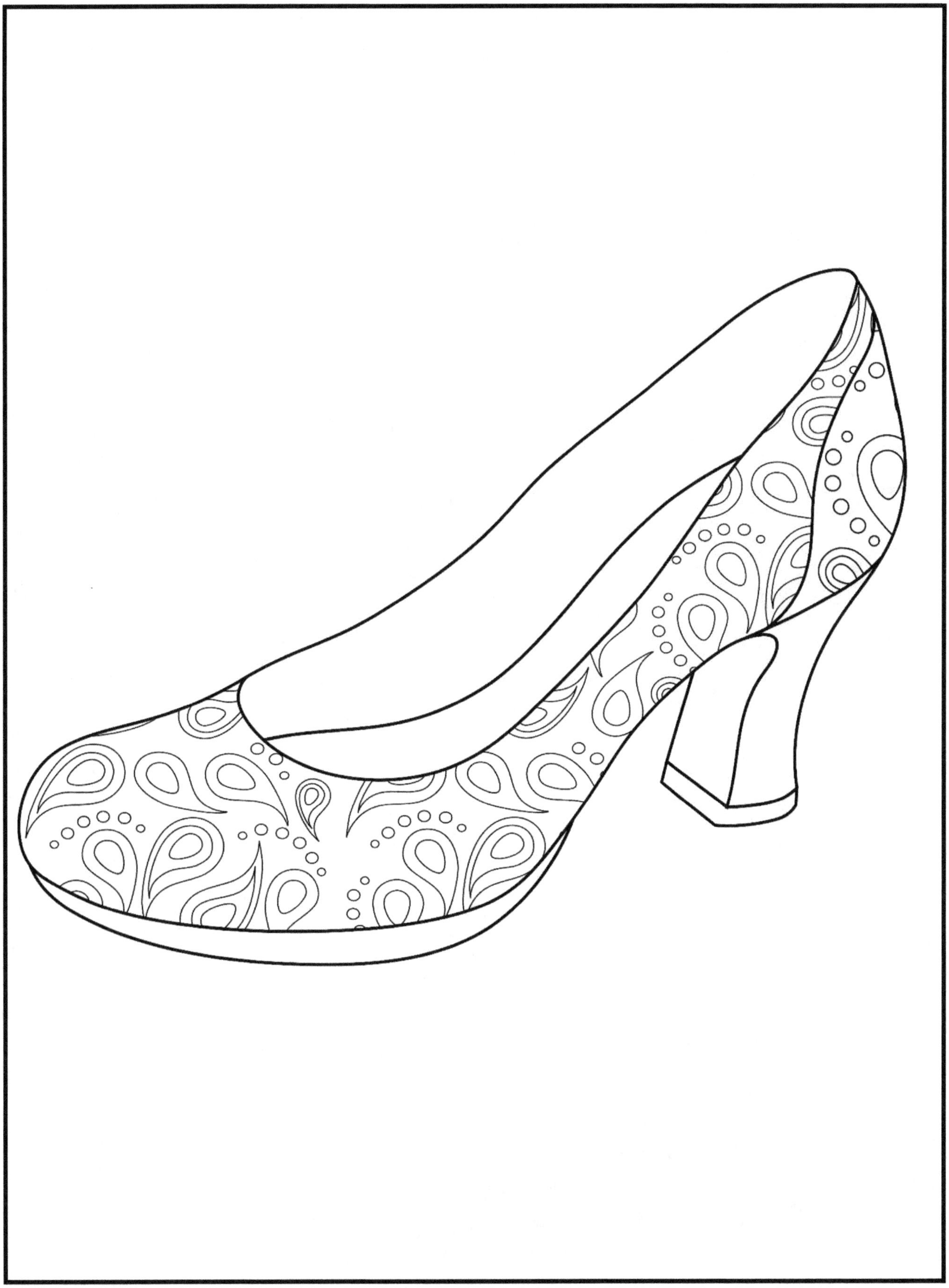

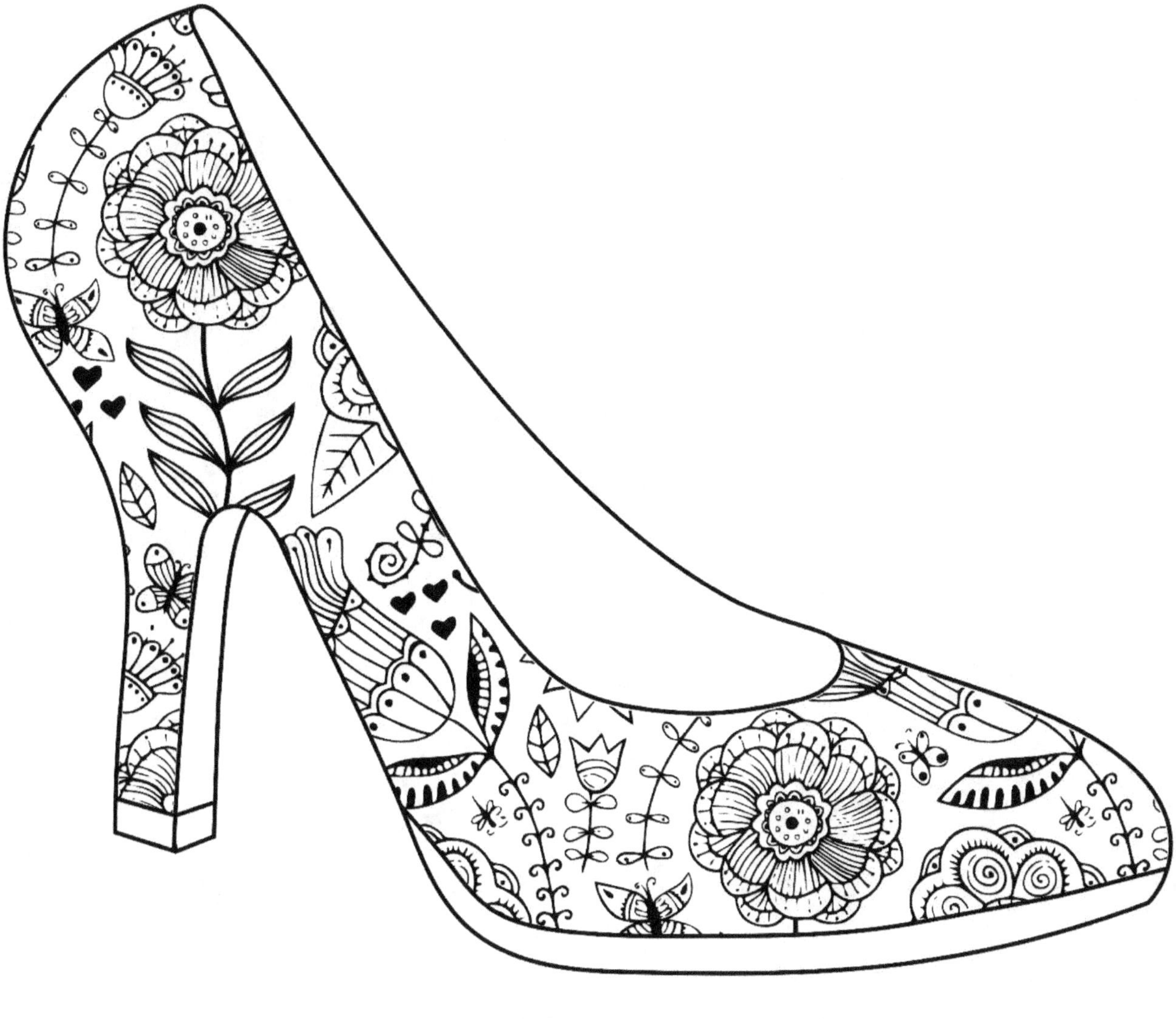

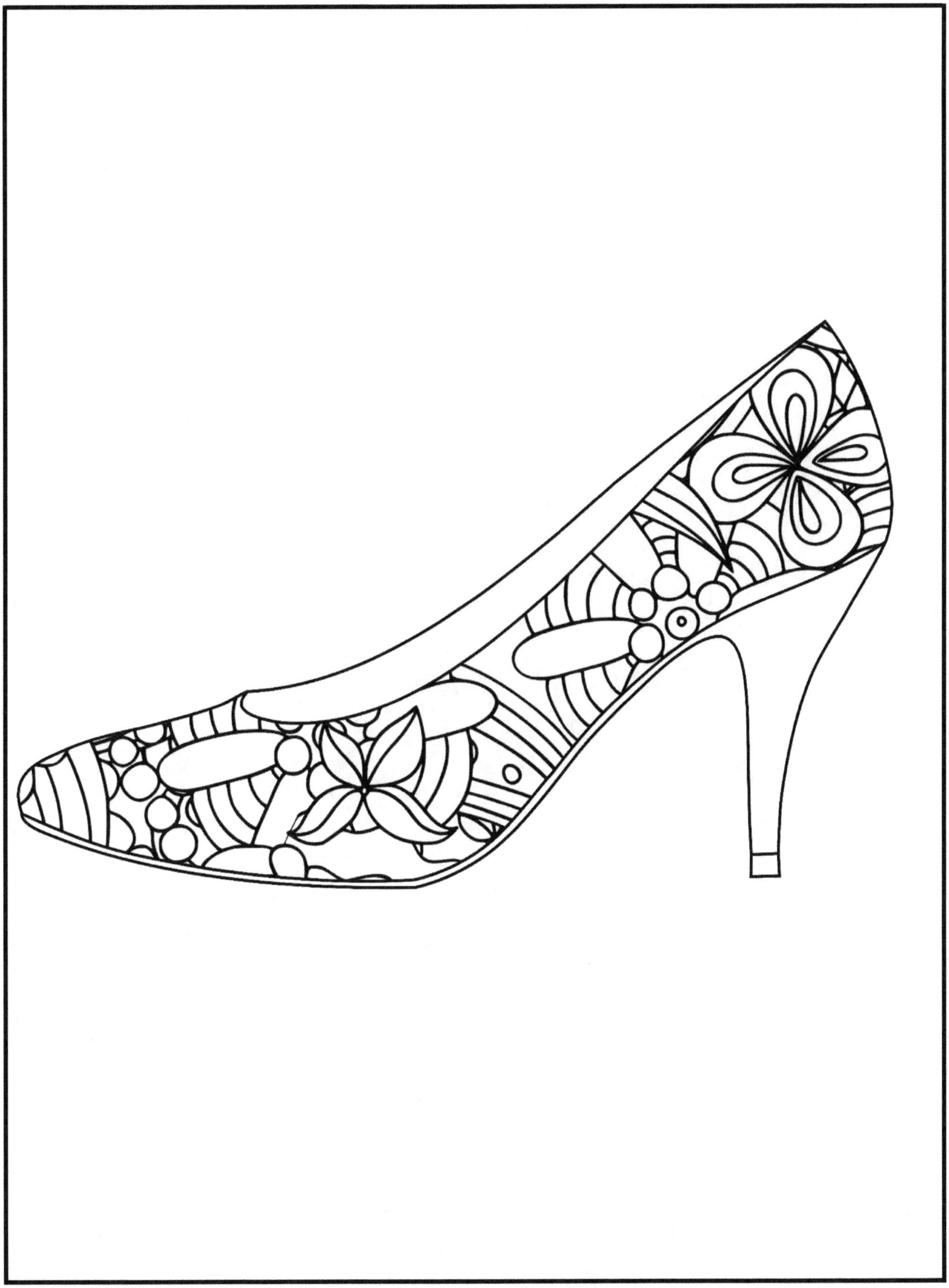

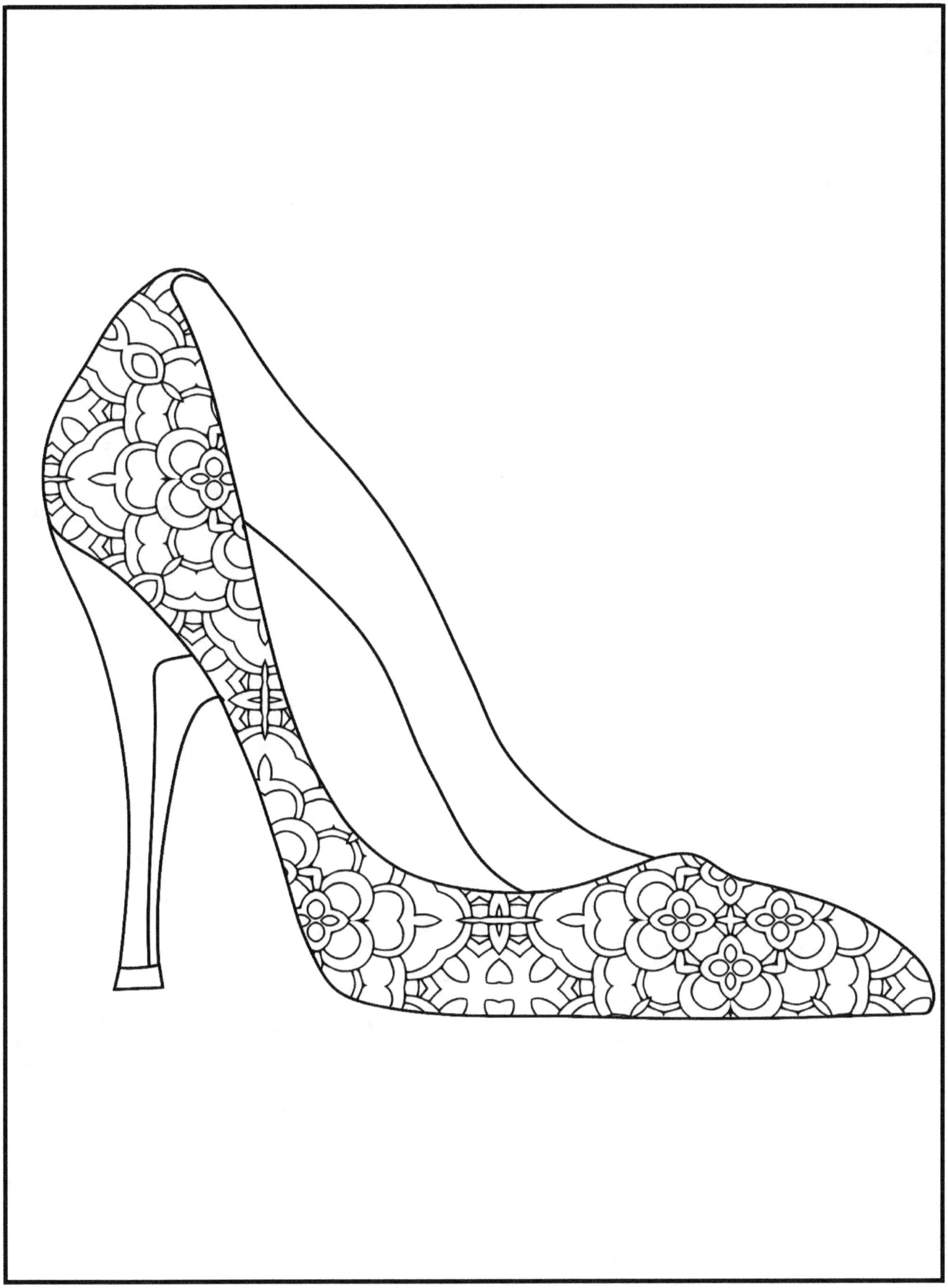

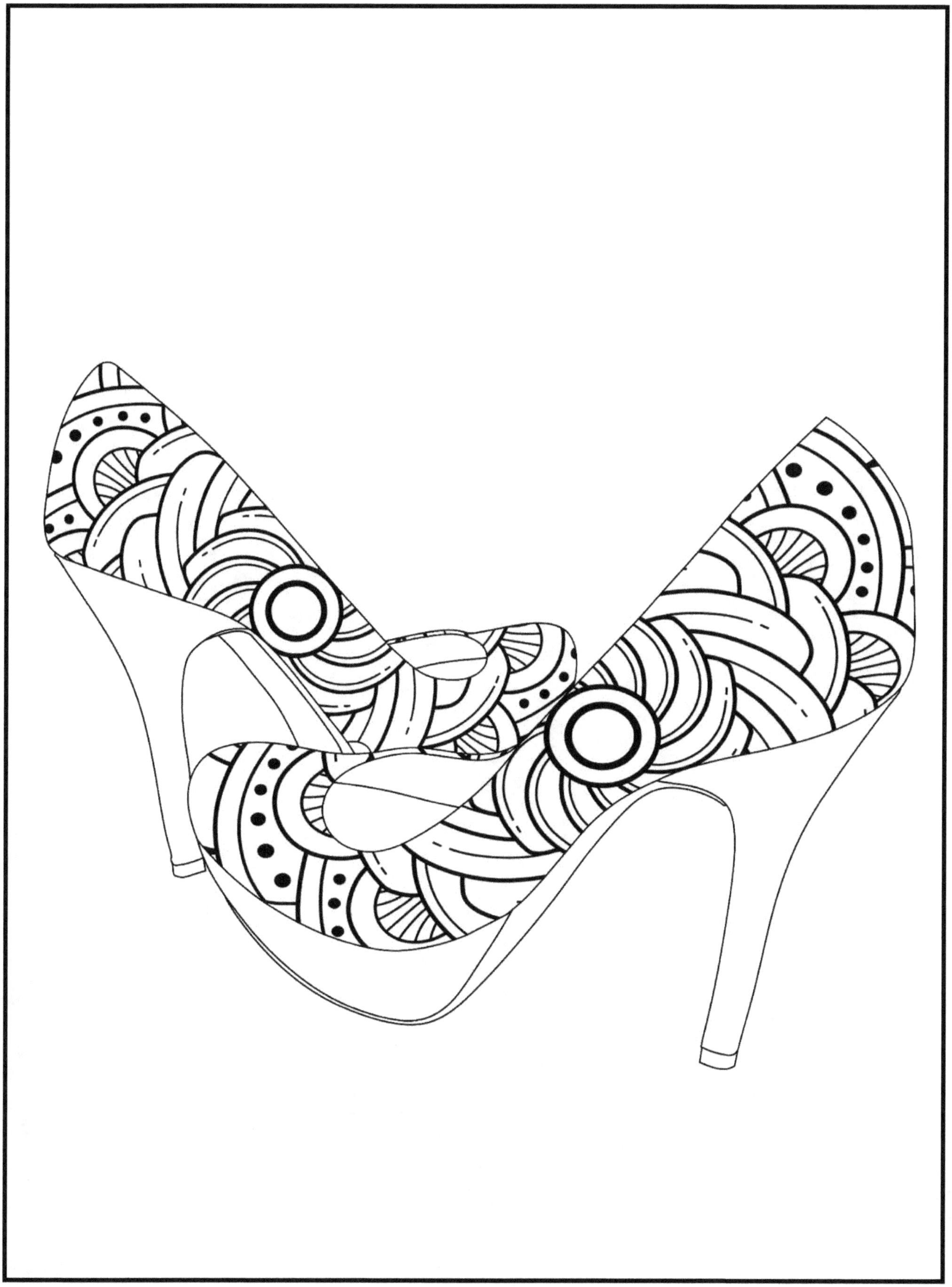

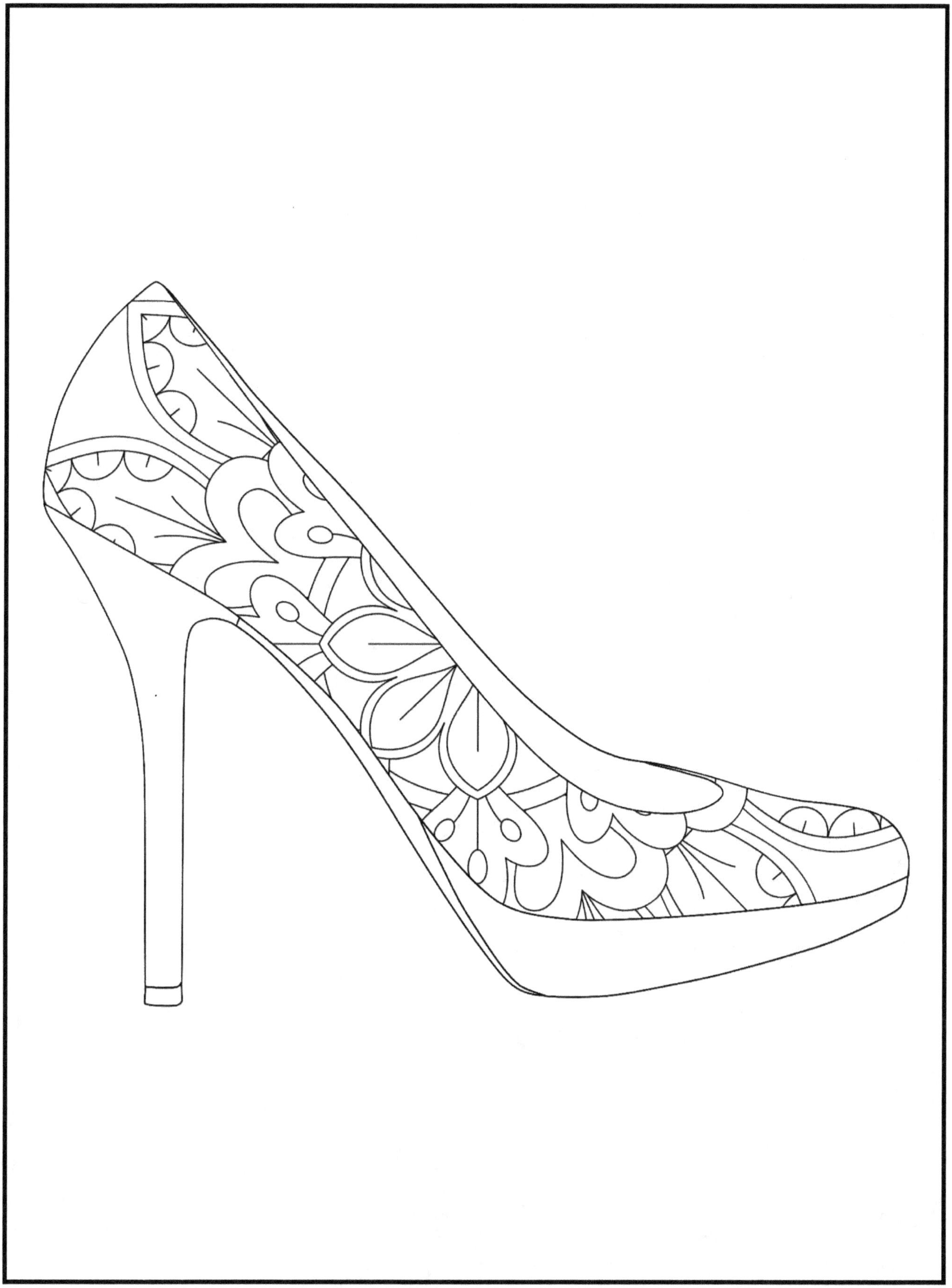

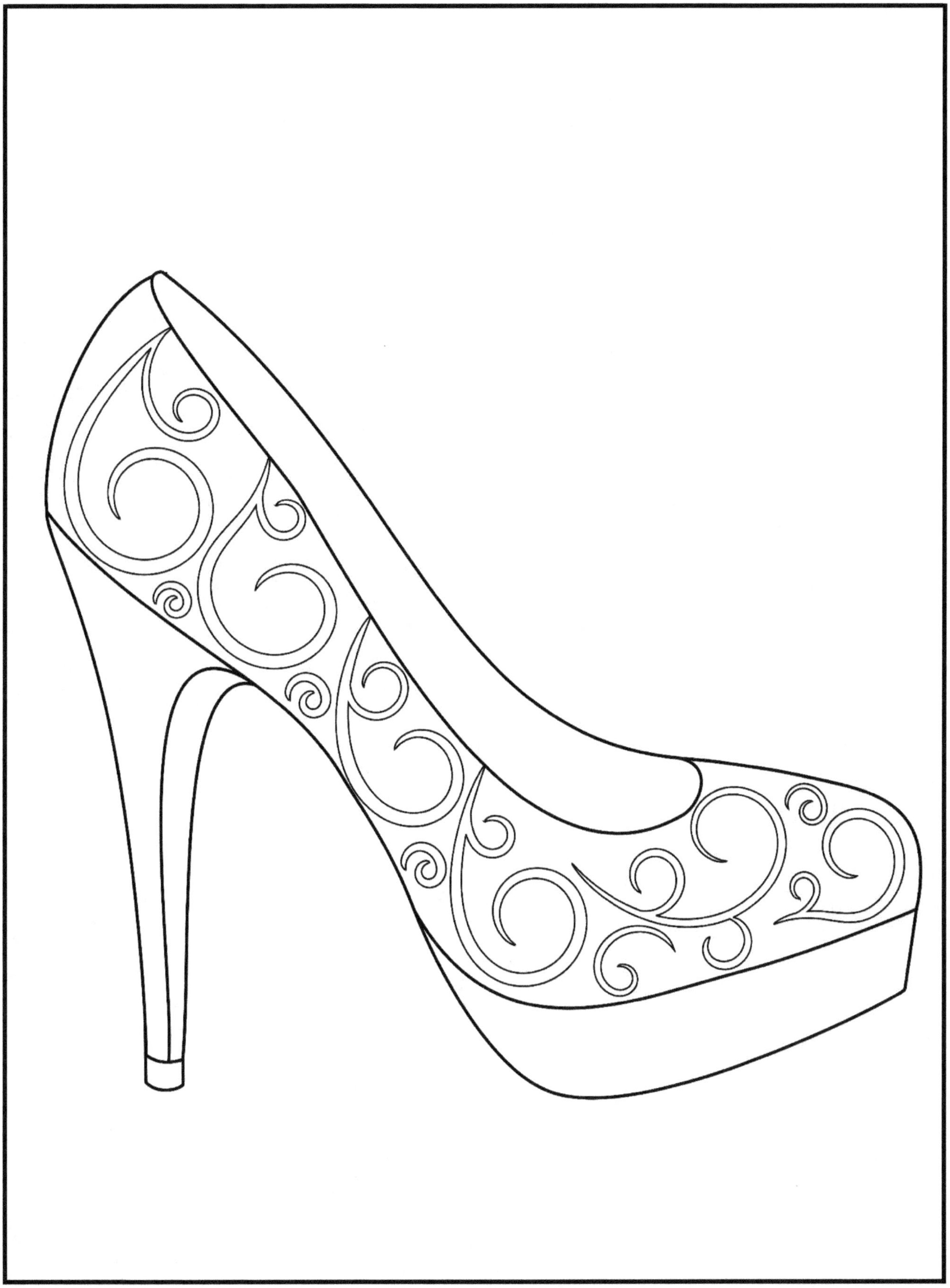

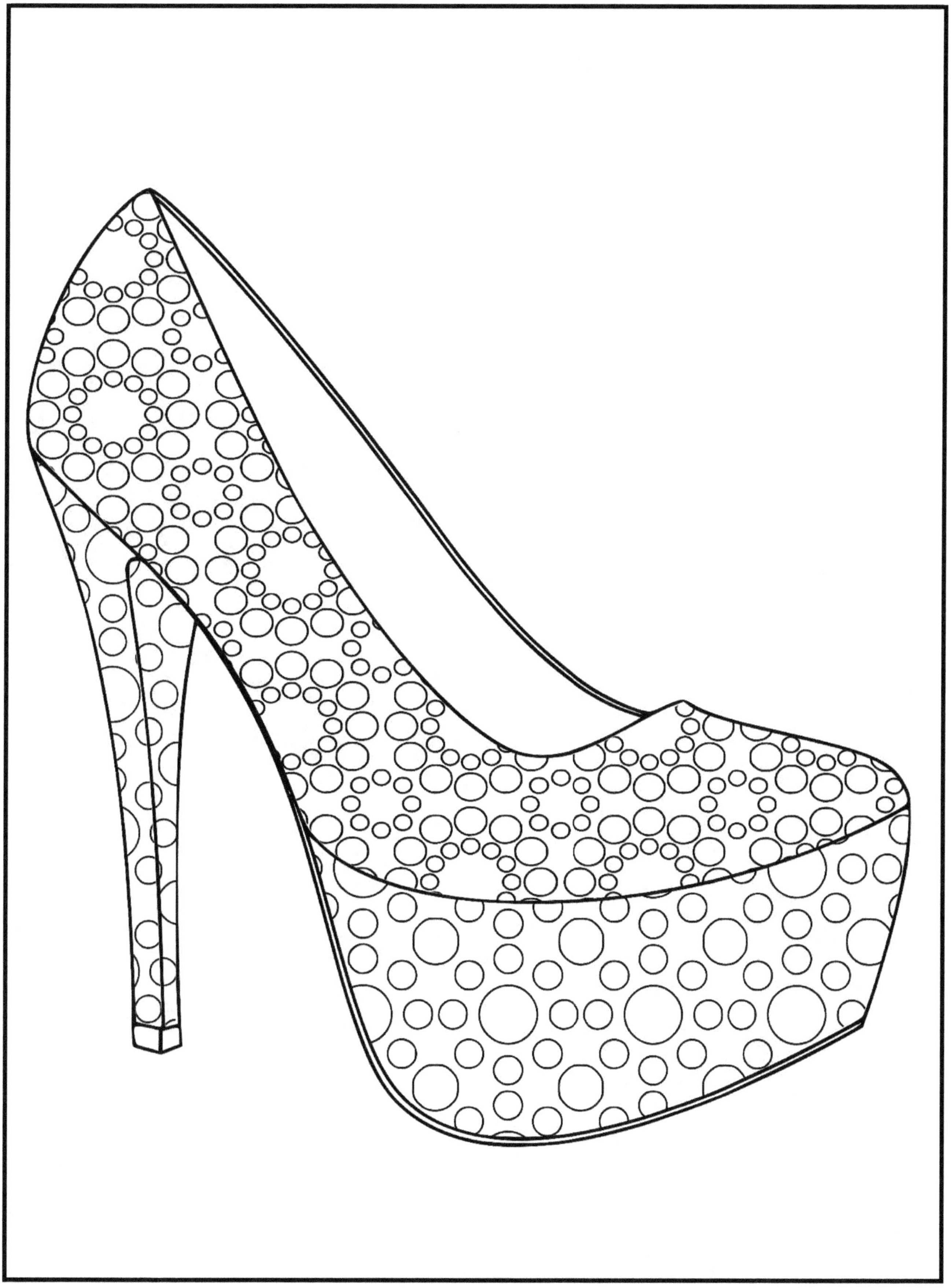

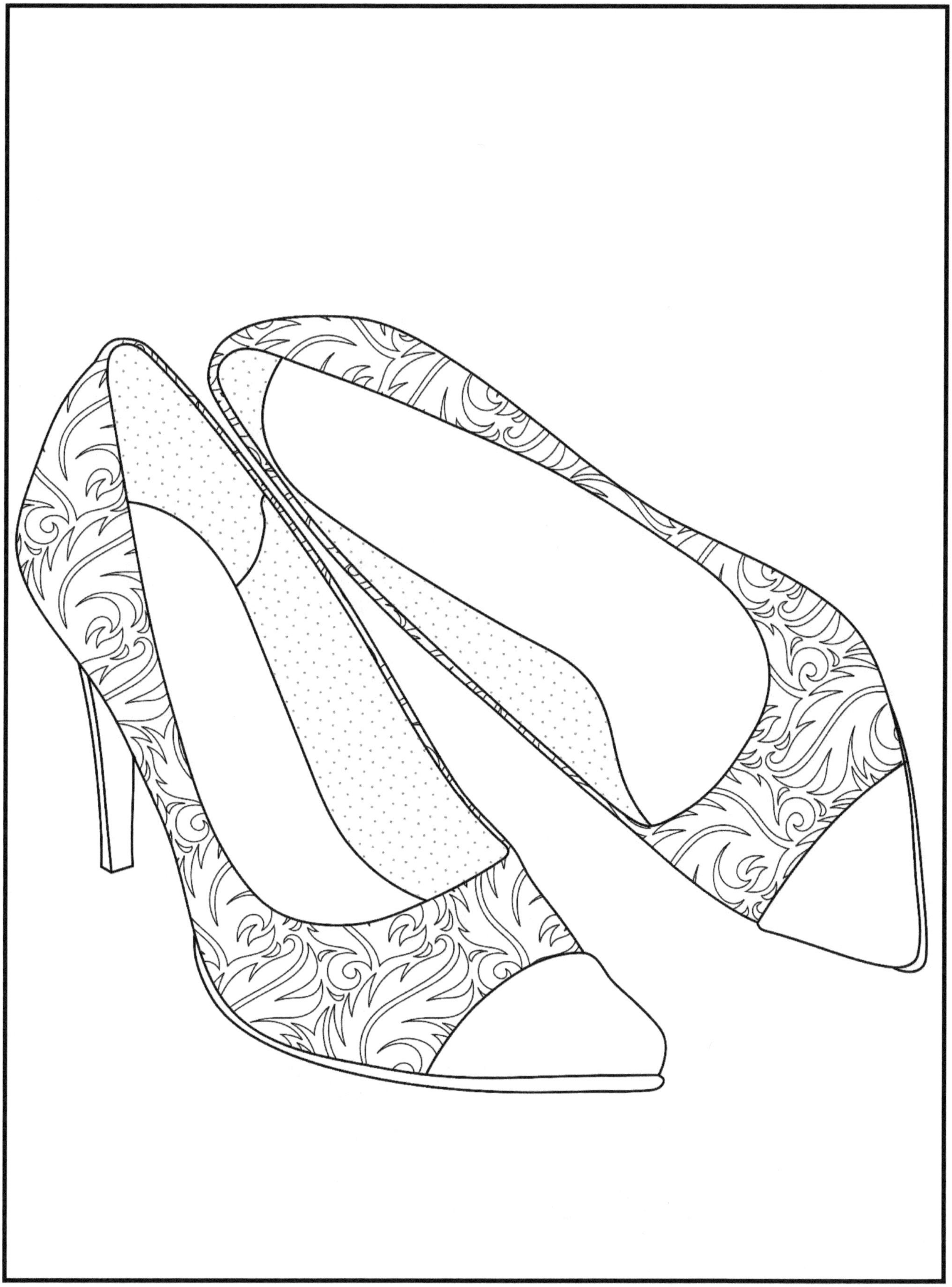

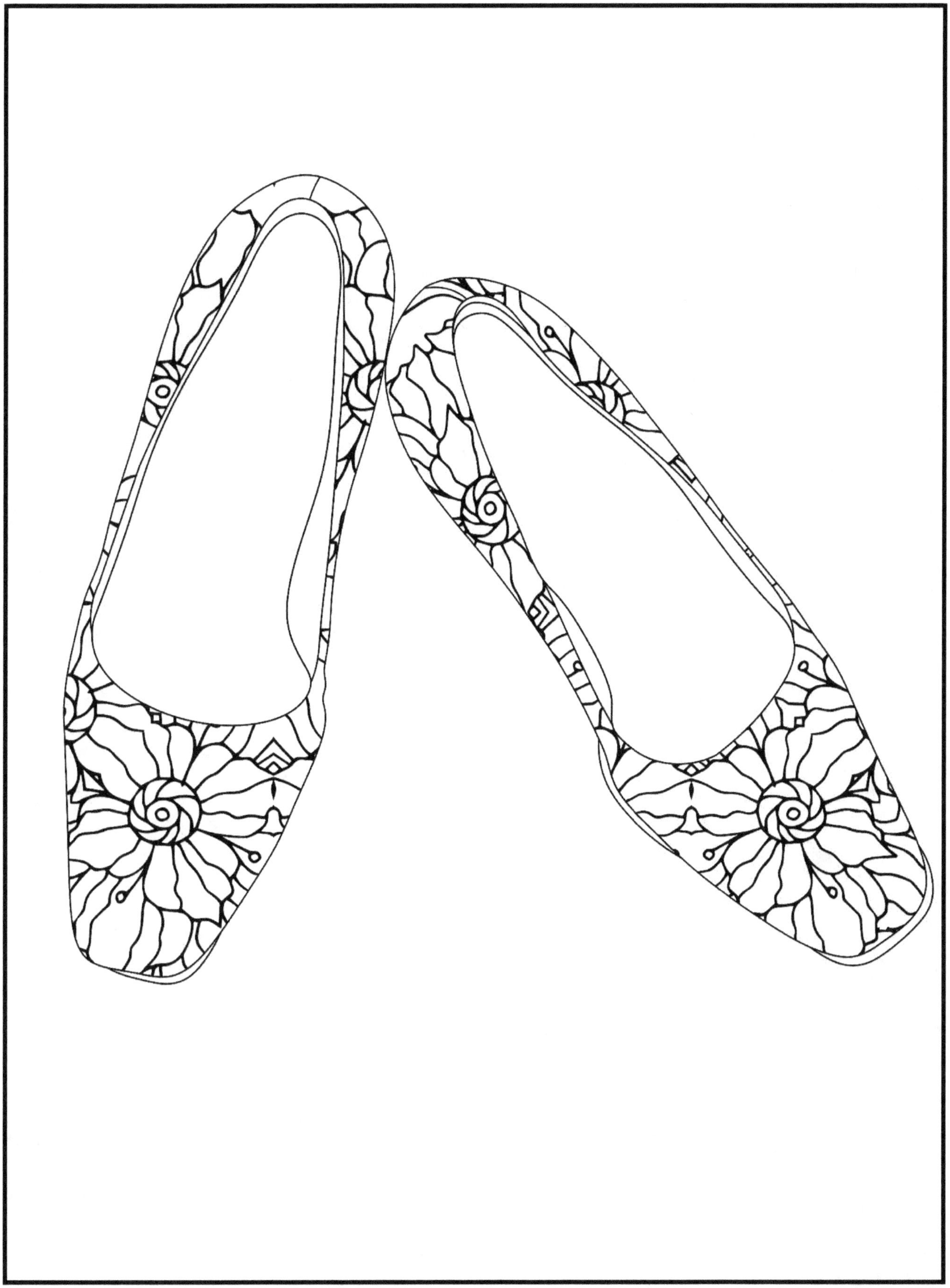

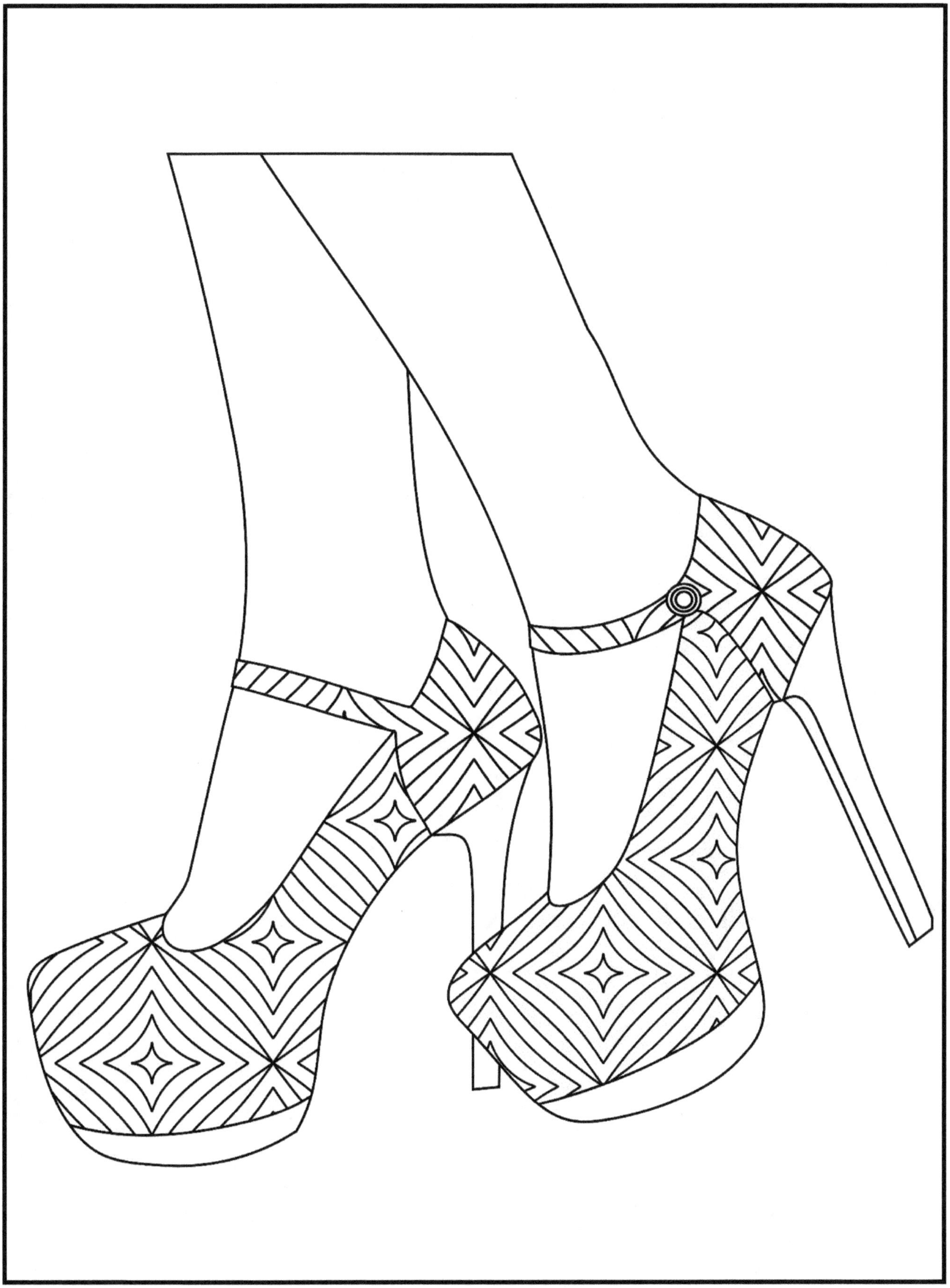

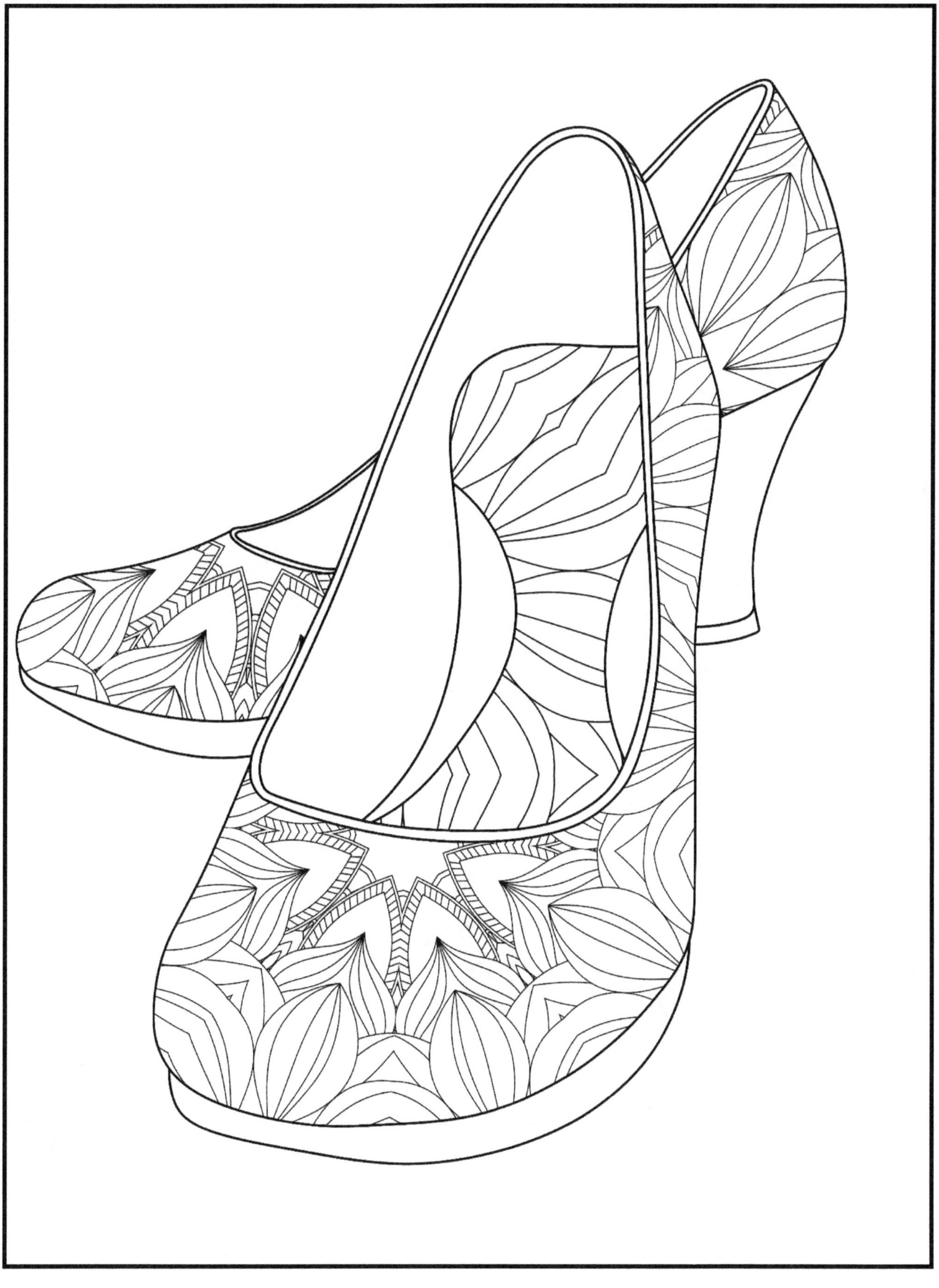

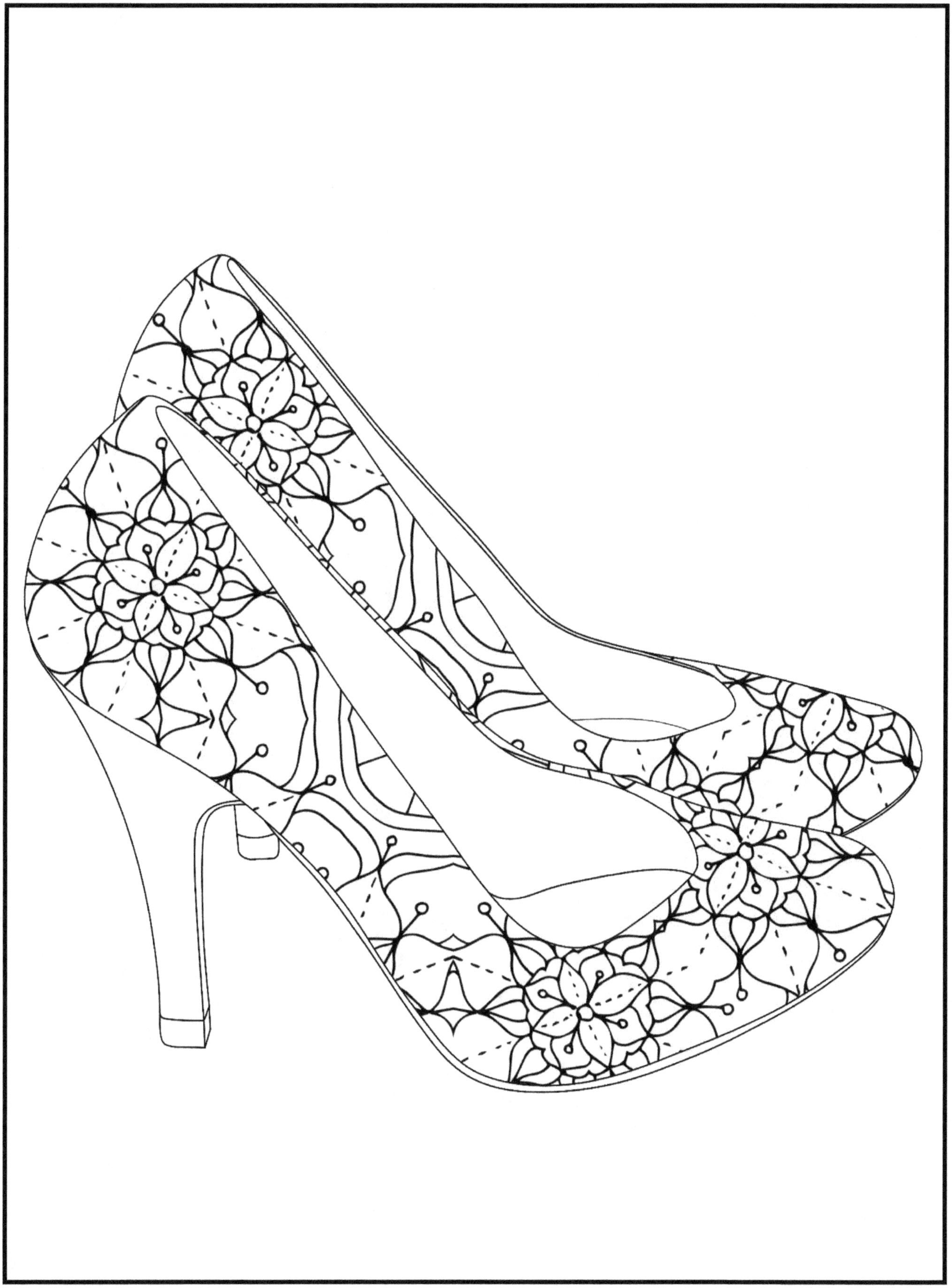

www.ingramcontent.com/pod-product-compliance
Lightning Source LLC
Chambersburg PA
CBHW081017170526
45158CB00010B/3069
* 9 7 8 1 0 7 0 5 7 0 4 1 9 *